TAKING A STAND AGAINST
NUCLEAR WAR

TAKING A STAND
AGAINST
NUCLEAR WAR

BY ELLEN THRO

Franklin Watts 1990
New York London Toronto Sydney

Illustrations by Vantage Art

All photos courtesy of: AP/Wide World Photo,
except Naval Photographic Center: p. 22.

Library of Congress Cataloging-in-Publication Data

Thro, Ellen.
Taking a stand against nuclear war / by Ellen Thro.
p.   cm.
Includes bibliographical references.
Summary: Surveys the history of the nuclear arms race, the
proliferation of weapons, and efforts by nations and individuals to
prevent their use.
ISBN 0-531-10922-4
1. Nuclear disarmament—Juvenile literature. [1. Nuclear
disarmament. 2. Nuclear warfare.] I. Title.
JX1974.7.T567   1990
327.1'74—dc20   89-24979 CIP AC

ACKNOWLEDGMENTS

My heartfelt thanks to the many people—students and adults—who shared their time, thoughts, materials, and actions with me as I wrote this book. The experience has left me particularly hopeful about the importance of peace to young people.

Special thanks to (alphabetically): Chris Backman, Eric Backman, Claudia de Albuquerque, Stephen Doyne, Leonore Duensing, Frank Garland (Physicians for Social Responsibility/San Diego), John Graham (Giraffe Project), Carol Jahnkow (Peace Resource Center of San Diego), Rick Jahnkow (Project YANO—Youth and Nonmilitary Opportunities), Michaelyn King (SEND—Students Embracing Nuclear Disarmament), Gloria McMillan, Stan Murphy, Pam Neumann (Peace Child Foundation), Vernon and Sue Nichols (Unitarian Universalist United Nations Office), Valentin Seveus (Citizen Diplomacy of San Diego), Jane Smith (Samantha Smith Foundation), Matt Starr, Lowell Strombeck (Citizen Diplomacy of San Diego), Chris Swan, Andrew Wang, Dolly Warden, Keith Warrick (University of San Diego High School), and Kerry Zurier (MEND—Mothers Embracing Nuclear Disarmament).

CONTENTS

TAKING A STAND AGAINST
NUCLEAR WAR

ONE

WHAT NUCLEAR WAR MEANS

Nuclear war. If the two words bring you frightening images of death, suffering, and destruction, you're not alone. Young people (and older ones) around the world share your fears.

As of 1990, the leaders of the two nuclear superpowers—the United States and the Soviet Union—have recognized these fears. The relationship has improved. But a buildup of nuclear weapons (the "arms race") has been underway since your parents were children. The possibility of nuclear war remains, as long as each nation has enough weapons to destroy the other's population many times over. In fact, neither government wants to get rid of all the weapons. Why? The present period of peaceful interaction between the two countries could disappear, as similar ones did in the 1950s and 1970s. The two nations could become active enemies again.

Government-to-government negotiations to reduce numbers of weapons are going on now. They are vital, of course, but they're just a first step to a warless world. Other action is needed. Would you be surprised to learn that each individual citizen can also help reduce the chance of war?

You, for instance.

How? First, you can begin to understand what's involved: what nuclear war's effects on human bodies and human societies are, why the arms race began, and the issues that must be settled before nuclear war can become impossible. This book will explain them.

Then, find out about people who have worked against war and—just as important—FOR peace. Peace isn't just something to think about at Christmas. Peace is an active process that grows as people work to bring it about. This book tells the stories of people who do this. Some of them are your age, and their stories are in their own words.

Finally, discover that YOU can make a difference. There are many ways to make your own contribution toward a peaceful world. The actions of people and groups can help shape our government's priorities, and build bridges to equally motivated people in the USSR. This book suggests some activities. As you read, you will probably think of others.

I hope you will discover that taking a stand against nuclear war can be an important and satisfying part of a life well-lived.

––––

No nuclear weapon has been fired at an enemy target since 1945. If we're careful, none ever will. But we have to be very careful, because there are so many of them. There are at least 60,000, enough to kill everyone in the world—eleven times over. They've been around for so long, some people think of them as just another fighting tool. But they're not. A nuclear war would be different from, and more terrible than, any other war.

Scientists have a clear picture of the deaths, illness, and destruction a nuclear war would bring—blasts and fires, radiation, epidemics, and shortages of water, food, and shelter. It would ravage the entire earth. It may even lead to the extinction of many species, including our own.

People usually ask, "What would it mean for my family and me?" That's a good question, not a selfish one. A nuclear war would touch everyone, so everyone should be concerned.[1-4]

THE EXPLOSION

A nuclear war could involve 5,000–10,000 megatons (MT) of nuclear weapons. A megaton is a million tons and refers to nuclear explosive power equal to a million tons of TNT. Most of the weapons used in such a war would be 1 MT or less.

Nuclear weapons cause two kinds of damage: *blast and fire,* just like a nonnuclear or conventional weapon, and *radiation.* The weapons can detonate (explode) either in the air or at ground level.

What follows describes the damage caused by a single 1 MT explosion on the ground. It's based on a computer simulation performed by scientific experts. Keep this in mind: Each city or other major target could be struck by many megatons, not just 1 MT.

At the moment of impact, a 1 MT weapon can dig a crater 1000 feet in diameter and 200 feet deep. This is called the "epicenter," or "ground zero" (see figs. 1 and 2). The explosion destroys

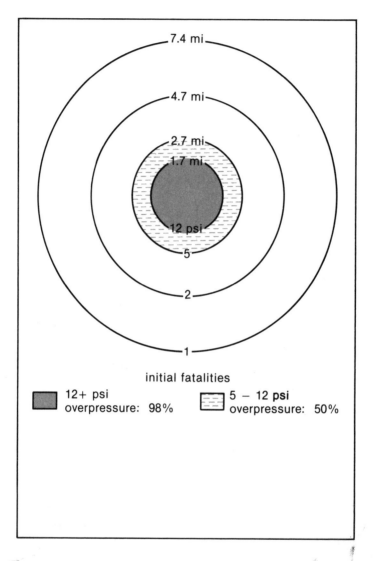

*Figure 1. Fatalities caused by a
1 MT nuclear weapon. Initial fatality
rate 7.4 miles (11.9 km) from ground
zero would be approximately 17%
(psi= pounds per square inch).*

everything within a half-mile of ground zero except concrete building foundations and bridge supports. The temperature will rise millions of degrees, creating a fireball—a sudden, powerful mass of hot air that ignites everything and everybody it touches.

In its first moments, the force of the explosion compresses the surrounding air to many times the normal 14.7 pounds per square inch (psi). This sudden "overpressure" and return to normal pressure kills people and crumples buildings. The effect is like using a plunger on a clogged drain.

The blast also generates winds measuring 500 miles per hour or more at ground zero. At 1¾ miles the overpressure is 2 psi, almost twice as strong as normal, and the wind more than 300 miles per hour. Ninety-eight percent of the people in this area will die almost immediately from the explosion, fire, and flying debris.

At 1¾–2¾ miles from ground zero, 50 percent of the population will die immediately, and another 40 percent will be injured. In all, within about 7½ miles of ground zero, almost 17 out of every hundred people will die immediately, and another 33 will be injured.[5,6]

THE RADIATION

A nuclear weapon produces large amounts of radioactive materials as it explodes. These mix with the pulverized earth and buildings and are swept up into the air. The wind then distributes them over the region. Some of this material, called "early fallout," drifts back to earth within a week or two. The rest is carried higher into the atmosphere. It

Bomb Effects—1 MT				
Minimum Immediate Fatalities (%)	none		5	
Minimum Immediate Casualties (%)	25		45	
Area (sq. mi.)	102.6		46.5	
Blast Overpressure (psi)	1–2		2–5	
Effect Peak Wind (mph)	70		163	
Distance from Ground Zero — mi	7.4	6.5	4.7	2.7
(km)	(11.8)	(10.5)	(7.6)	(4.4)
Structural Damage: U.S. Cities		Little damage to buildings. A few controllable fires.	Most severe fire hazard area. 5% of buildings ignited; half of all buildings destroyed within 24 hours, without firefighting.	Large buildings: no windows or interior partitions. Contents of upper stories blown into streets.
Other Effects				Winds strong enough to blow people out of buildings. 50% of people standing up can be killed by 3.5 psi winds.

Figure 2. Effects of a 1 MT ground explosion in the first hour.

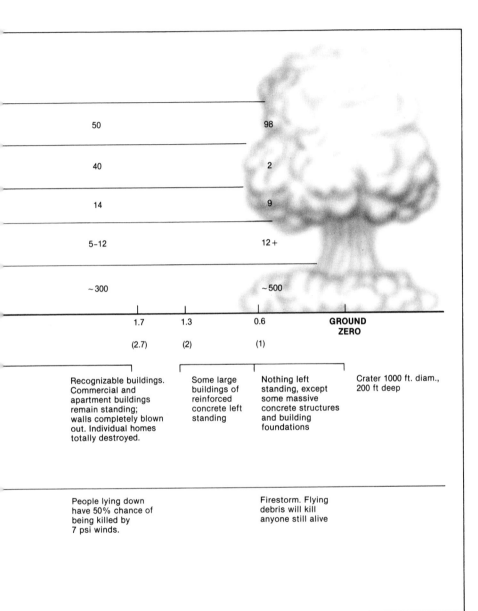

50			98
40			2
14			9
5–12			12+
~300			~500

| 1.7 | 1.3 | 0.6 | **GROUND ZERO** |
| (2.7) | (2) | (1) | |

| Recognizable buildings. Commercial and apartment buildings remain standing; walls completely blown out. Individual homes totally destroyed. | Some large buildings of reinforced concrete left standing | Nothing left standing, except some massive concrete structures and building foundations | Crater 1000 ft. diam., 200 ft deep |
| People lying down have 50% chance of being killed by 7 psi winds. | | Firestorm. Flying debris will kill anyone still alive | |

becomes part of the global air circulation and falls to earth over the next several years. As with all air pollution, the fallout pattern depends on wind-speed and direction.

Figure 3 (p. 19), based on the simulation, shows how far early fallout spreads and how deadly it is. In the simulation, the wind blows steadily at 15 miles per hour in a single direction during the first seven days after detonation. Everyone remaining in an area 90 miles long and 10 miles wide down-wind receives lethal doses of radiation. Half of the people between that area and 155 miles downwind die from the radiation dose they receive during the first week.

Many targets may be bombed at once in a war. Figure 4 (page 20) shows what happens if 1 MT bombs hit Boston, New York City, and Washington, D.C., with the wind blowing out of the north-east. Fallout from Boston covers Providence, Rhode Island. New York's fallout kills as far away as Philadelphia. The 30- , 90- , and 155-mile circles let you see where the fallout would go if the winds blew from any other direction.

Of course, in a real situation, the wind will vary in speed and direction, spreading the fallout differently. In the 1986 Chernobyl, USSR, reactor accident, for instance, the wind first spread the radiation northward, toward Scandinavia. Later it turned south, into Italy. Rain or snow would also change the bomb fallout pattern, washing it to earth earlier.

Maps and computer models can only sketch the possibilities for death and destruction from nuclear war. Photographs from Hiroshima and Nagasaki, Japan, bombed in 1945, show the depth of

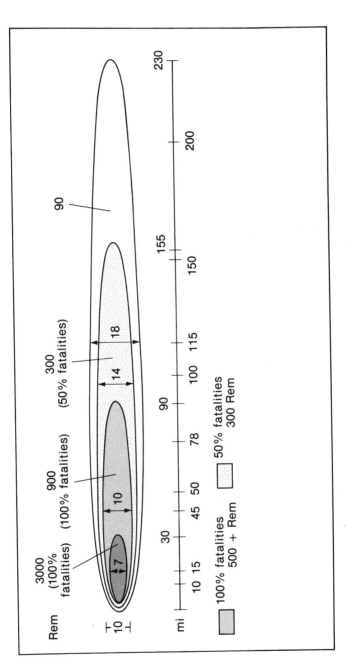

Figure 3. Fallout-related fatalities from a 1 MT ground explosion.

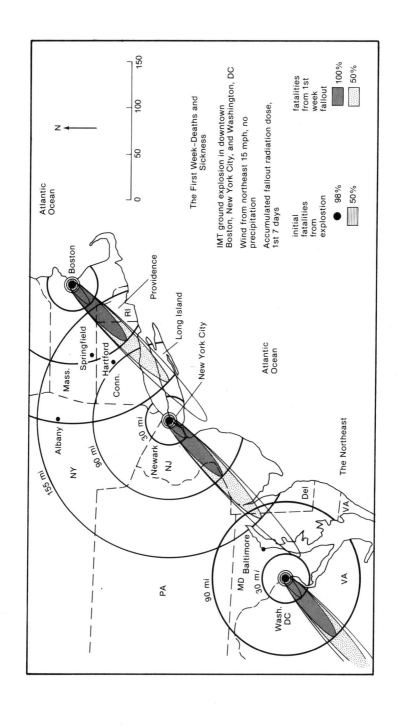

The First Week–Deaths and Sickness

1MT ground explosion in downtown
Boston, New York City, and Washington, DC

Wind from northeast 15 mph, no
precipitation

Accumulated fallout radiation dose,
1st 7 days

initial
fatalities
from
explostion

- 98%
- 50%

fatalities
from 1st
week
fallout

- 100%
- 50%

The Northeast

Atlantic
Ocean

Atlantic
Ocean

N

0   50   100   150

Boston

Providence

RI

Springfield

Hartford

Mass.

Conn.

Long Island

New York City

Albany

NY

90 mi

155 mi

30 mi

Newark
NJ

PA

90 mi

MD Baltimore

30 mi

Wash.
DC

Del

VA

VA

the tragedy: a burned wristwatch; a dying woman, looking like a skeleton loosely covered by shredding skin; the burned and broken bodies of passengers thrown from their streetcar as the explosion occurred; the charred body of a little boy lying face up in the rubble, about half a mile from ground zero; the human-shaped shadow on a wall, marking where a soldier 2¼ miles from ground zero was vaporized. Survivors called themselves "living ghosts."[1,3,5,6]

RADIATION SICKNESS

The bombing of Hiroshima and Nagasaki brought the world a new disease. It's called "radiation sickness." Like poison, the more radiation entering your body, the sicker you get. If the dose is too large, you die.[1,3,4] The early symptoms are the same in everyone. Within a few days, people lose their appetites (anorexia) and feel exhausted. They become nauseated. They begin vomiting and have diarrhea.

In the United States, radiation dose is measured in rads. These units measure the amount of radiation energy the body absorbs. If your body as a whole receives less than 150–200 rads, you may or may not have symptoms of radiation sickness. Even if you do, you will almost certainly recover.

Figure 4. Deaths and sickness from 1 MT ground explosions in Boston, New York City, and Washington, D.C.

Atom bomb damage in Nagasaki, Japan, at conclusion of World War II, September 1945.

The computer simulation used a unit called the rem, which measures the effect of radiation on body tissue. For the most common type of fallout radiation, 1 rem = 1 rad.

The largest dose, 5,000 rads or more, will disable your brain (central nervous system) and heart. You will die within the first two days after the attack. If your dose is 1,000–5,000 rads, you will have more severe forms of the early symptoms. You will bleed heavily (hemorrhage), lose body fluids (dehydration), and be an easy target for infections. You will die within the first two weeks after the attack.

If your dose is between 200 and 1,000 rads, you may seem to recover after a week or so. But within a month you will become seriously ill again. Your bone marrow, which produces blood cells, will be damaged. If you receive over 450 rads, you will die within three to eight weeks after the attack. If you get between 200 and 450 rads, you may survive. These numbers are approximate. People's bodies respond to similar doses of radiation differently. Weight, age, and general health all affect your ability to resist.

There are other symptoms of radiation sickness, too. These depend on the dose received by specific body organs. Radiation can affect your skin, lungs, eyes, and reproductive system. Your hair may fall out. If your skin received less than about 300 rads, hair will probably grow back. If the dose was over 700 rads, it probably won't. You may get a lung disease, pneumonitis, and it may be fatal.

It's hard to say how many people with intermediate forms of radiation sickness will live or die. In Japan, medical help arrived from other cities almost immediately. In modern nuclear war there may be no outside medical help. If there is any, it will probably be too little to treat the vast numbers of sick people.

Doctors and nurses are just as likely to be killed or injured or to get radiation sickness as anyone else. Hospitals are just as likely to be destroyed as other buildings. If hospitals remain standing, people may not be able to get to them, or their equipment may be useless. After the Chernobyl accident, medical specialists from all over the world went to help the people who had radiation sickness. Those who were the sickest died in spite of the help. This level of treatment will be impossible after nuclear war.[1-4]

THE FIRST YEAR—
WILL SURVIVORS FREEZE
IN THE DARK?

Scientists have been studying the effect of nuclear war on people, animals, plants, and buildings since 1945. But no one thought of nuclear war's effect on the earth's weather until the 1980s. Some respected scientists believe the changes would be so profound that they invented a name for it— "nuclear winter."[7,8] Other equally respected scientists think the changes would be much less severe.

What is nuclear winter? It wouldn't be caused by the earth's position in orbit, as the season of winter is. But its effects would be similar and even more extreme. Nuclear bombs cause fires that generate large amounts of dust and smoke. This can change the weather over large regions, or even globally. They absorb some of the sun's rays and bounce others back, away from the earth. Enough very small particles, evenly distributed, don't leave spaces in between to let the sun's rays through.

This situation actually occurs regionally during forest fires and dust storms. Major volcanic eruptions throw large amounts of dust high enough into the sky to circle the earth for a year or more (just as fallout does). In 1815, the Tambora volcano in Southeast Asia produced enough dust to create winterlike conditions in North America, Europe, and elsewhere through the entire year of 1816. It snowed in summer, and crops failed because of low temperatures and lack of light. People called it "the year without a summer" or "eighteen-hundred-and-froze-to-death."

Even a major nuclear war would probably occur within only a day or two, suddenly creating vast amounts of dust and smoke. Buildings, parks, crops, prairies, and forests will burn out of control. There are about 1.5 billion tons of oil and gas in storage worldwide. These would burn. Wells would rupture, feeding more fires. One estimate is that 5,000 MT of explosives will inject more dust and soot into the atmosphere in a few days' time than during an entire ordinary year—over 225 million tons. The great heat of the surface and the much cooler sky will draw particles as high as nineteen miles into the air, just like smoke up a fireplace chimney.

The computer simulation for nuclear winter projects that during the first six weeks probably only 1 percent of the normal amount of sunlight will reach the Northern Hemisphere. By the end of five months, this should improve to 25 percent of normal light level, and by eight months after the war, to 50 percent of normal light level. No matter what season of the year, postwar temperatures will plunge far below zero—as much as seventy-seven Fahrenheit degrees below normal during the first four months. This will improve to "only" forty-one degrees below normal temperatures nine months after the war, and five degrees below normal by the end of the first year.

The actual temperatures could hover between $-60°$ F and $-10°$ F at the end of the first four months, between $-28°$ F and $+26°$ F after nine months, and from $20°$ F to $38°$ F by the end of the first year.

The nuclear-winter simulation concludes that:

- Buildings and clothing won't be able to protect people against the arctic-style cold.
- Fresh water will be frozen solid.
- There will be no new crops.
- Darkness and polar temperatures will soon kill virtually all plant life that depends on photosynthesis. Many species of animals will soon follow.
- The extreme cold, plus the depressing effect of extended darkness, may speed up people's deaths from radiation or other sickness.

Will nuclear winter follow a nuclear war? Perhaps not. Some scientists think the estimate of 225 million tons of smoke may be too high. Even some who accept the estimate don't think the effects will be so extreme. Meteorology—the science of weather—is not exact. Local or regional weather could greatly change global patterns.

THE WAR'S LONG-TERM CONSEQUENCES

Even without nuclear winter, many terrible things will be happening at the same time. People will be ill or dying from radiation sickness, burns, and blast effects. Sanitary systems won't work, so sewage will go untreated. In many places, there will be no running water, so toilets won't flush. During the coldest period, the ground will be too frozen for people to dig graves. Dead bodies of people and animals will decay, becoming breeding places for diseases and insects. Most people who survive will do it without medical care.[1-8]

The survivors could also be attacked by any of a long list of diseases: cholera, dysentery, food poisoning (salmonellosis), infectious hepatitis, typhoid fever, meningitis, tuberculosis, typhus, diphtheria, polio, rabies, whooping cough, influenza, pneumonia, blood poisoning (tetanus), bubonic and pneumonic plague, strep throat. Even "minor" diseases could kill large numbers of survivors. Many survivors—perhaps one-third—will be too emotionally disabled to function effectively.

Among the victims of the war may be the ozone layer high in the stratosphere, which protects the earth from the sun's harmful ultraviolet (UV) radiation. This is the same layer of the atmosphere that is now threatened by aerosol sprays and other chemicals. In the postwar world, the more sunshine that reaches the earth, bringing heat and light, the larger the dose of UV radiation.

Agriculture as we know it may no longer be possible. Seed supplies and fertilizer may not be available. There may be no gasoline for farm equipment. Cattle and horses that might be used instead may have died or been eaten before agriculture has a chance to resume.

Rainfall will be contaminated by fallout for at least two years. As it mixes with the soil and surface waters, it will deposit its radioactive burden. In the first few years, fallout will contaminate crops directly, worldwide. After that, crops will take it up through the roots. This will assure continuing high levels of radioactivity in war survivors, increasing the chance of cancer and genetic damage.

But for most survivors the greatest food-related health problem will be malnutrition—the lack of anything to eat. Lack of transportation will keep city people from getting grain that is stored in rural areas. Other stored food will be unavailable or quickly used up. It will probably contain enough radioactivity to hasten the deaths of people who eat it. Even far-off Third World countries that now depend on food from the developed world will face mass starvation.

The environment may never be the same as it is now, even far from the bombed areas. Radiation affects the growth and reproduction of each plant and animal species differently. This will mean different dominant plants and altered predator-prey relationships.

What will life be like ten years after the war? Will modern economies revive? Or will people either produce their own food, clothing, and fuel or barter for it? What about education and entertainment? They may take place locally, if at all. Medical care? Probably minimal.

Will there be running water, telephones, electricity, cars, or airplanes? Technology as we know it may not be redeveloped for a long time. Travel will be difficult. Some experts speculate that daily life may resemble that in the poorest countries today. Democracy itself could become a thing of the past as governments struggle to ensure survival and share limited resources.

TWO

HOW NUCLEAR WEAPONS WORK

In August 1945, the United States had two nuclear weapons. They were named, respectively, "Little Boy" and "Fat Man." Little Boy was used on Hiroshima, Fat Man on Nagasaki. Today the U.S. is believed to have 30,000 nuclear weapons—certainly too many to name.

The destructive power of the first two weapons came from the splitting of atoms (fission); uranium atoms for Little Boy and plutonium for Fat Man. Within a decade, fission (the atomic bomb, or A-bomb) alone was no longer considered powerful enough.

The next generation of weapons used thermonuclear or fusion reactions, releasing much greater power by combining hydrogen atoms (hydrogen bomb, or H-bomb). Today's thermonuclear weapon uses a small fission weapon as a trigger to begin the fusion. The combination of fission and fusion gives nuclear weapons their explosive power and their ability to kill with radiation.

Today's "bomb" is the "warhead" of a complete weapons system. Scientists design the system to be large or small, with varying explosive and radiation power, depending on military needs. Then they match it to a method of delivering it to the target—field weapon, missile, or airplane.

WHAT NUCLEAR ENERGY IS

All matter is composed of atoms—materials that can't be subdivided without losing their basic identity. The core of an atom is its nucleus. Each nucleus contains one or more positively charged protons and usually one or more neutrally charged neutrons. The more protons and neutrons it has, the heavier the atom is. Around each nucleus is one or more negatively charged particles or pulses of energy called electrons.

Energy holds protons, neutrons, and the nucleus itself together. Energy also holds the electrons in the vicinity of the nucleus. Whenever changes occur within the atom, energy is incorporated or released. In fact, on the atomic level, matter and energy are interchangeable. This was one of the fundamental discoveries leading to the splitting of the atom. Another one was the discovery that it takes more energy to hold together a very heavy or very light atom than a medium-weight atom.

The number of protons in its nucleus defines the atom of any element. Each hydrogen atom, for instance, contains one proton, while uranium contains ninety-two protons (fig. 5, page 32). Most elements come in several varieties, called "isotopes," depending on the number of neutrons in the nucleus. Isotopes are identified by the total number of protons and neutrons the nucleus contains.

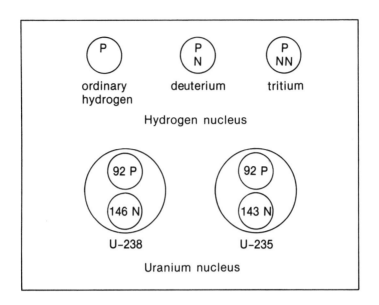

*Figure 5. Isotopes of hydrogen and uranium.
U-235 was the first fissionable isotope.*

Hydrogen, which is the fuel of thermonuclear weapons, is identified by its single proton. This makes it the lightest element. Hydrogen (symbol H) has three isotopes: Ordinary hydrogen, called hydrogen-1, has one proton and no neutrons; its nucleus is the same thing as a proton. Hydrogen-2 (usually called deuterium, or D) has one proton and one neutron. And hydrogen-3 (tritium, or T) contains one proton and two neutrons. Uranium (symbol U), one of the fission fuels, is the heaviest natural element. It also has several isotopes, the most common being U-238, with 92 protons and 146 neutrons. U-235 has 92 protons and 143 neutrons.[1]

FISSION WEAPONS

Energy holds atoms together and is released when atoms or nuclei are changed. Adding neutrons, changing neutrons to protons, and releasing electrons are some of the ways an atom can change. Fission is a special type of change, involving splitting the nuclei of certain very heavy isotopes into two approximately equal parts. So much energy is released that it takes only 12.5 pounds of fissionable material to produce a 1 MT nuclear explosion. U-235 was the first fissionable isotope.[1]

Uranium

Splitting a U-235 nucleus requires insertion of a neutron (fig. 6). As the neutron strikes, the nucleus splits into two similar clusters of elements, releasing energy and more neutrons. These neutrons in turn may cause more fission of other nuclei, at an

Figure 6. A neutron is used to split the U-235 nucleus, releasing energy and more neutrons.

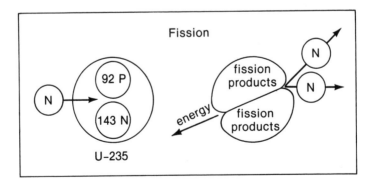

increasing rate. If so, the result is a sustained, or "chain," reaction. No chain reaction can take place without two things: (1) a steady supply of neutrons and (2) a minimum amount of fuel in any specified shape or density, called a "critical mass."

In nature, free neutrons move at random, interacting randomly with other matter. If you have a chunk of U-235, eventually a neutron will come along that is able to split one of the nuclei. But sustained nuclear energy requires a reliable supply of neutrons to sustain the chain reaction.

For a weapon to be effective, the chain reaction must be instantaneous. So it must have a less-than-critical mass of fuel until the moment of detonation. In Little Boy, the fuel was kept in two pieces, which were fired into each other for the detonation. In Fat Man, the fuel was kept subcritical by its density. At the moment of detonation, explosives placed all over its surface were fired at the same time. This imploded (collapsed) the fuel to greater density and a critical mass. It was like compacting an air-filled volleyball into the size and density of a softball.

Plutonium

U-235 isn't the only fissionable isotope. Plutonium-239, the other fuel used in fission weapons, is an element created by scientists. It doesn't exist in nature. Plutonium (symbol Pu) is manufactured (or "bred") from U-238 in specialized reactors. A three-stage process is involved (fig. 7, page 35).

As you just saw, a nucleus of U-238 has 92 protons and 146 neutrons. The first stage is addition of a neutron. This changes U-238 into a different uranium isotope, U-239 (with 92 protons

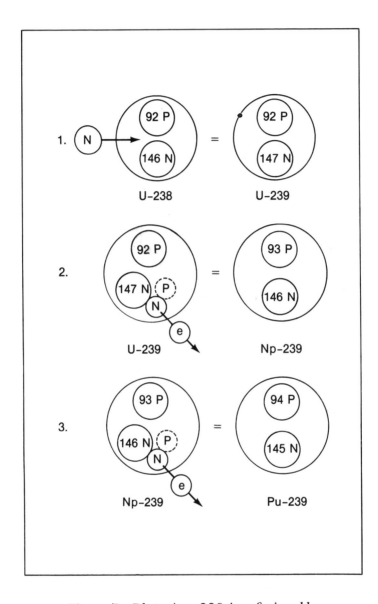

Figure 7. Plutonium-239 is a fissionable isotope that doesn't exist in nature and must be "bred" by a three-stage process.

and 147 neutrons). But this addition makes the new nucleus unstable.

For the second stage, after less than half an hour, one of the neutrally charged neutrons releases an electron (negatively charged) and becomes a positively charged proton. The nucleus now has 93 protons and 146 neutrons. Since uranium must contain only 92 protons, the nucleus has become the core of a new element, called neptunium (Np). The isotope is Np-239.

The final stage occurs about two days later, when the same process occurs: An unstable Np-239 neutron releases an electron, turning into a proton. The nucleus now has 94 protons and 145 neutrons and is an isotope of another new element, this time Pu-239. Pu-239 is a very long-lived material that is both fissionable and radioactive.

FUSION WEAPONS

You can think of fusion as the opposite of fission. In fission, energy is released through the splitting of a very heavy nucleus. In fusion, energy is released by the joining of very lightweight nuclei.

A thermonuclear weapon works by fusion of two hydrogen nuclei. This creates one helium nucleus, releasing energy in the process. The details are government secrets. The hydrogen may be two deuterium nuclei, two of tritium, or one of each. A variation may involve changing a slightly heavier element, lithium, into helium and tritium. If the lithium is incorporated with deuterium, the reaction will release energy and also allow a deuterium-tritium reaction, producing additional energy. A weapon's fusion reaction requires a very high temperature, which is produced by the fission trigger.

Neutron Bomb
The neutron bomb is a small or tactical H-bomb. Its fission trigger is designed to release large amounts of lethal neutrons without destroying much property. This deliberately increases the radiation received by soldiers or other people nearby. The U.S., the USSR, China, and France have such weapons in their arsenals.

BOMBS AND RADIATION

In Hiroshima, as many as 100,000 people—40 percent of the population—died from the explosion and radiation from a single 0.15 MT bomb. The explosive power was only about one-eighth that of a 1 MT weapon. At Nagasaki, a 0.21 MT bomb killed 26 percent of the population. The explosions and fires, terrible as they were, were similar to those caused by conventional weapons. Earlier in World War II, we used fire bombs on Tokyo, Japan, and Dresden, Germany. What made Hiroshima and Nagasaki unique were the radiation effects.

Scientists began studying the survivors just a few weeks after the bombs struck. Japanese and American scientists have been studying them ever since—people who lived through the attacks, those whose mothers were pregnant with them, and their descendents. What the scientists have learned in Japan makes up the core of the world's information about the effects of weapons-generated radiation on humans. Knowledge also came from studying goats, sheep, and other animals that were deliberately exposed to atmospheric testing in the 1950s and early 1960s.[1-4]

During one of the tests in 1954 at Bikini atoll, in the Pacific, humans were accidentally exposed to a bomb's immediate fallout. These were crewmen of a Japanese fishing boat, the *Lucky Dragon*, that mistakenly sailed into the test area. They all developed radiation sickness, and the captain died. The survivors were treated, and their progress was carefully monitored.

Some former U.S. service veterans believe their health was damaged by radiation exposure when they entered the Japanese cities shortly after the attacks or from weapons tests in Nevada or in the Pacific. Some residents of southern Utah also believe their health problems result from weapons testing in Nevada. None of these people were examined regularly over the years, so it is hard to evaluate their charges.

Every person and other living organisms were shaped in part by radiation from the sun, soil, and rocks. This is known as "natural" or "background" radiation. But the body's tolerance for radiation is very narrow, and too much can cause damage. How much radiation is too much? Scientists assume that any amount beyond background changes the way the body's cells and organs function. Changes can include the way the cells reproduce, turning normal cells into cancer cells. If it damages the DNA, the cells' genetic material, it can cause birth defects or other problems in children the person has later.

Nuclear reactions produce four types of radiation: alpha, beta, gamma, and neutron. For weapons effects, gamma and neutron are the most important. They all harm living tissue the same way, by disrupting cellular activity. As the radiation moves through tissue, it ionizes atoms within the cells. This means it separates the nuclei from the outer electrons. For this reason, it is called "ionizing radiation."

Alpha radiation consists of the nuclei of helium atoms. Beta rays are electrons. Gamma rays are similar to X rays. These all harm living tissue directly. Alpha rays create damage internally. Beta radiation can damage the skin or internal organs when taken in with food, drink, or air. Gamma rays are harmful to both the skin and internal organs.

Neutrons work indirectly. When they are released by the explosion, they make the air, soil, and other materials radioactive—what is called "induced radioactivity." These materials then emit gamma rays as well as some alpha rays. Anyone going near ground zero afterward will be exposed to this radiation. Some of these reactions continue to take place for years. And some of the materials they create, such as cesium-134 and cobalt-60, give off radiation for several years.

Radiation from fallout may also work on the skin or internally, from contaminated air, food, and water. The main long-term sources of radiation from fallout are cesium-137 and strontium-90. They lodge in the body, where they give off gamma radiation for more than thirty years. Cesium can remain in any part of the body. Strontium is very similar to calcium and accumulates in the bones. Iodine-131 is also an important early fallout product, which goes to the thyroid gland.

U.S. WEAPONS PRODUCTION
AND DELIVERY SYSTEMS

A nuclear weapon is the end product of many steps, some of them hazardous: design and research, uranium mining, plutonium production, refining of uranium ore, extraction of plutonium from the reactors, production of explosives and electrical systems, fuel fabrication, assembling of weapons, testing, and performing research on safety and transportation.

Uranium mining is commercial. All the other operations are carried out at sixteen facilities owned by the U.S. Department of Energy (DOE).[5] Table 1 (page 41) shows which activities are carried out at each facility. If you look at the map (fig. 8, page 42), you might find one located near you.

Little Boy and Fat Man were dropped from airplanes. Today almost half of U.S. nuclear weapons are still carried by bombers. For the majority, the method of delivery is the missile—a rocket fired from land, air, or sea at a specific target.[6] The three options of bomber, ground-based missile, and sea-based missile are sometimes referred to as "the triad." (The USSR has similar weapons in all categories.)

Bombers are classified as "strategic" because their 7000-mile range will let them go directly to targets in the Soviet Union. They are believed to carry both bombs and missiles that can be aimed at ground targets.

Missiles are classified in two ways: whether they have an intercontinental, intermediate, or short *range* and whether their *function* is strategic or tactical. Intercontinental ballistic missiles (ICBMs) are

TABLE 1. WHERE WEAPONS ARE MADE

		RESEARCH/ DEVELOPMENT	FUEL MATERIALS	WEAPONS COMPONENTS	WEAPONS ASSEMBLY	WEAPONS TESTING	HEALTH/ SAFETY
Feed Materials Production Center	Fernald, Ohio		X				
Hanford Site	Washington		X				
Idaho National Engineering Laboratory	Idaho	X	X				
Kansas City Plant	Missouri			X			
Lawrence Livermore National Laboratory	California	X					
Los Alamos National Laboratory	New Mexico	X					
Mound Facility	Ohio			X			
Nevada Test Site	Nevada					X	
Pantex Facility	Amarillo, Tex.				X		
Pinellas Plant	Florida			X			
Portsmouth Uranium Enrichment Complex	Ohio		X				
Rocky Flats Plant	Denver, Colo.			X			
Sandia National Laboratories and the Inhalation Toxicology Research Institute	New Mexico			X			X
Sandia National Laboratories, Livermore	California	X					
Savannah River Plant	South Carolina		X				
Y-12 Plant	Oak Ridge, Tenn.		X	X			

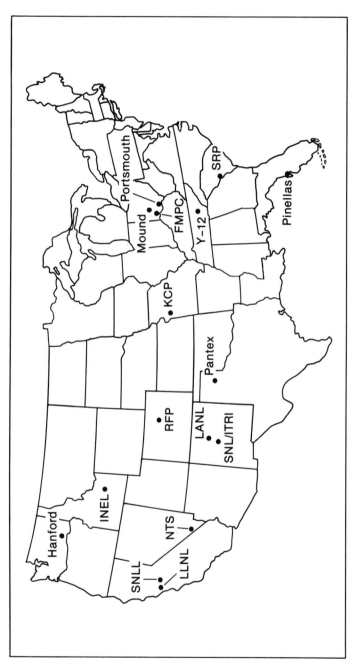

Figure 8. Map of U.S. nuclear weapons production sites (see Table 1 for complete names).

land based and are also called "strategic" missiles. They have ranges of about 7000 miles. From the U.S. they can reach targets throughout the USSR in a half hour. They are based in underground silos throughout the U.S. and are all targets for Soviet ICBMs (which can also make the trip in half an hour). Strategic missiles launched from submarines at sea are known as submarine-launched ballistic missiles (SLBMs). Their ranges are shorter—up to about 4300 miles.

Intercontinental missiles can have single or multiple (as many as ten) warheads attached to the rocket carrier. A multiple-warhead missile is called a MIRV (pronounced "murv"), or multiple independently targetable reentry vehicle. Such a missile is said to be MIRVed. When the missile is in mid-flight, the warheads are released, one at a time. Each warhead can be aimed at a different target, so MIRVed missiles are much more efficient than single-warhead missiles. On the other hand, it takes only one enemy hit to destroy all the warheads on a MIRVed missile that is in its silo or just starting its flight.

"Tactical" nuclear weapons have shorter ranges. They are intended for use within a region, such as Europe or Asia, or even in individual battle zones in support of ground troops. They include artillery shells, bombs, air-to-air missiles (fired from one airplane at another), and sea mines (in harbors, for instance). The "cruise missile" is a small land, air-to-ground, or sea-launched missile that can maneuver as easily as a jet plane. It has a range of about 1,500 miles.

In many cases, the missiles themselves (without the warheads) and the launching equipment can be used with either nuclear or nonnuclear weaponry.

Submarines are one "leg" of the U.S. strategic triad, which also includes bombers and ICBMs. Shown here is the Ohio, a Trident nuclear submarine.

An unarmed Tomahawk cruise missile undergoing testing in Northern Maine. Cruise missiles are tactical (shorter-range) nuclear weapons.

For instance, the navy's Tomahawk cruise missile can be used as a strategic nuclear weapon or a tactical conventional weapon. Such choices give the president, other decision makers, and military commanders more flexibility in considering military responses. It is believed that nuclear weapons can only be launched on the authority of the president and the secretary of defense.

THREE

THE COLD WAR — FORTY YEARS OF MAD

The "Cold War" refers to hostility between the United States and the USSR involving everything except direct fighting. The two nations have been each other's chief enemies since the end of World War II in 1945. The result has been an arms race and the buildup of an arsenal of 60,000 nuclear weapons—30,000 for us, 30,000 for them. The fire-power includes the missiles, airplanes, and submarines to launch them. There are also nonnuclear (conventional) weapons and defenses against each other's possible use of chemical and biological weapons.

The Cold War also consists of real wars, involving "surrogate" nations like El Salvador and Nicaragua. Or the war can be between one of us and a third nation. The U.S. fought the Soviet-backed North Vietnamese. The USSR fought the U.S.-backed rebels in Afghanistan.

The Cold War hasn't turned hot because the two countries have maintained a "balance of terror" by following the policy called mutually assured destruction (MAD). Why are the U.S. and USSR enemies? The reasons are historical and political.

THE U.S.-USSR RIVALRY

The two countries became rivals as far back as the early nineteenth century, when they both were interested in the northern Pacific basin. Russia (as the USSR was called then) had settlements in the Pacific Northwest and even claimed land in North America until they sold it to the U.S. in 1868. Today "Russian North America" is the state of Alaska.

Western Europe and Russia mistrusted each other in the nineteenth century because of religious and cultural differences. When the Revolution of 1917 turned the Russian Empire into the Communist Soviet Union (USSR), mistrust increased. In the 1920s and 1930s, Communist parties formed in most western nations, including the United States. There were "Red Scares"—fears of Communist terrorists. On the eve of World War II, the USSR and its dictator, Joseph Stalin, signed a peace pact with Germany's dictator, Adolf Hitler. The pact was broken when Hitler invaded the Soviet Union.

As a result, the Western European nations and the USSR joined forces. Then Japan started the Pacific war, and the U.S. became involved. Japan and the USSR were regional rivals and had fought several earlier wars. The Soviet Union now declared war on Japan, making the U.S. and the USSR allies in both Europe and Asia. But the USSR had to devote all its resources to the fight against Germany. It couldn't be active against Japan at the same time.

By 1945, however, the Allied victory was in sight. Germany surrendered in the spring. The Japanese were defeated everywhere but on their home islands. The U.S. faced a hard choice: either an invasion of Japan that might require years of fighting and cost many U.S. lives or a quick end to the war by using a new weapon, the atomic bomb.

The U.S. had developed the bomb because American scientists believed the Germans were developing one. The thought of a nuclear weapon in Hitler's hands convinced President Roosevelt that the U.S. should have one first. The war was over in Europe before the weapon was ready.

Some experts now think that Japan would have surrendered at the threat of an invasion. But in August 1945 the U.S. still considered Japan a very strong enemy. President Truman decided to use the bomb—twice.

The president had two primary reasons. One was to avoid the invasion. The other was that the USSR was expected to start fighting against Japan later in the year. If this happened, it would probably take over the large parts of Japan's empire that lay along its border and become much more dominant in the Pacific Basin. But Japan surrendered a few days after the second bomb was dropped.

By the time World War II ended, the USSR was demanding large pieces of territory under the upcoming peace treaty. It was clear that the next big rivalry would be between the U.S. and the USSR. The USSR had begun expanding in the late 1930s, when it annexed the Baltic states of Estonia, Latvia, and Lithuania and took territory from Romania and Finland. As the Allied armies moved eastward through Germany in 1945, one of their objectives was to be sure that the Soviet army didn't "liberate" territory beyond what was always considered "Eastern" Europe.

In spite of the USSR's expansionism, the U.S. and other Western nations felt militarily superior, because we had the bomb. But in August 1949, the Soviet Union developed its own nuclear bomb, earlier than expected. The arms race was on.

THE BEGINNINGS OF MAD

The principle of "mutually assured destruction," aptly abbreviated MAD, was first proposed in 1946 as a way to deter (discourage) nuclear war between the U.S. and the USSR.[1] Since then, three defense doctrines have competed in determining U.S. policy: (1) military superiority, (2) arms reduction, and (3) arms limitation or deterrence. The supporters of each have always believed their doctrine is the one that will prevent nuclear war.

Military superiority is the ability to launch enough nuclear weapons to destroy the enemy with a "first strike" and to successfully strike back if the enemy attacks first. If this doctrine is to prevent war, the enemy must be aware of this capability.

Arms reduction involves negotiating to actually cut the numbers of weapons, or certain types of weapons, and destroy some of them. Total disarmament is the goal of some people in this camp, but it is considered extremely unlikely.

Arms limitation or deterrence is what keeps MAD from boiling over into war. It is the official U.S. policy and means each side is just strong enough to strike back and cause massive damage if the other side attacks first. This balancing act means we build weapons for the purpose of never using them.

Deterrence involves two kinds of limitations—on new technology and on the number of weapons. In practice, it has allowed the arms race to continue, but in a controlled way. The limits are achieved by diplomacy and treaties. It is supposed to be only temporary, though it has lasted for forty years. Supporters consider it a more rational approach than the doctrine of military superiority. Many believe it is the only rational approach. Most of the treaties that the U.S. and USSR have negotiated have been to maintain the stability of this system.

THE 1940s AND 1950s—
THE RACE FOR SUPERIORITY

The U.S.'s nuclear bombing of Japan also brought calls for the strict control of this new "ultimate" weapon. Many people thought that its existence would make war obsolete. Others saw the possibility, but only if the bomb were under strict international controls.

The U.S. made the first proposal to control nuclear weapons in 1946. It was called the Baruch Plan, after Bernard Baruch, the U.S. representative to the United Nations Atomic Energy Commission. The plan called for international control of the entire process of producing nuclear energy, from mining to manufacturing of weapons. Eventually, it would include destroying all nuclear weapons.

The year 1948 brought a series of confrontations between the U.S. and the USSR. When the war ended in Europe, Germany had been divided into five administrative areas. The four major Allied powers each controlled one zone—France, Great Britain, the U.S., and the USSR. Berlin, Germany's capital, lay inside the Soviet zone but was governed jointly by the four countries.

The USSR was supposed to allow French, British, and U.S. auto and truck traffic across its zone into Berlin. But in 1948 the Soviets blockaded the highway. The other nations considered responding militarily. Instead, they began a round-the-clock airlift of supplies that lasted for almost a year, until the USSR lifted the blockade. Also in 1948, Soviet-backed Communist governments took control of Poland, Czechoslovakia, Romania, Yugoslavia, Bulgaria, and Albania.

In 1949 the Soviet Union tested its own first nuclear weapon.

A few months later, a Communist government took over in China. Reaction in the U.S. was angry and intense, leading to the biggest Red Scare of all. Sen. Joseph McCarthy, a conservative from Wisconsin, thought Communists were influencing every section of U.S. society. A heated debate ensued about who "lost" China.

Now the U.S. seemed to have two Communist enemies—China and the USSR. In 1950, Communist-controlled North Korea invaded U.S.-supported South Korea. The U.S. responded militarily, followed by China. The Korean Conflict was the first nuclear-era war.

Presidents Truman and Eisenhower both considered using smaller nuclear weapons to support ground troops but didn't. Practical reasons, such as protecting troops, prevented it. So did public opposition when President Truman mentioned the

*When the Soviet Union blockaded the road
to West Berlin in 1948, during a tense period
of the "Cold War," the other allies responded
with a massive airlift of supplies.*

Senator Joseph McCarthy of Wisconsin spearheaded investigations of alleged communist influence in many areas of American life during the early 1950s.

idea at a news conference. Allies may also have urged the U.S. not to use them. And an American attack on China or Chinese troops might have caused the Russians to retaliate. But President Eisenhower wanted both China and the USSR to be aware of the possibility. It was part of his belief in the threat of "massive retaliation" as a way of maintaining superior strength.

Meanwhile, research was producing more awesome weapons. By the mid-1950s, the U.S. and the USSR had hydrogen bombs. Radioactive fallout first became an international issue at the time of the H-bomb tests at Bikini atoll, in the South Pacific, in 1954. The atmospheric explosions were twice as powerful as expected, and the fallout was massive. Press accounts focused on the radiation sickness and one death on the *Lucky Dragon.* But as the contamination circled the globe, it was detected worldwide. A similar test in the Soviet Union resulted in radioactive rain falling on Japan.

Military superiority was the main goal in both countries. Even so, President Eisenhower and, apparently, Soviet premier Khrushchev wanted to slow the arms race by stopping weapons testing. Various nations proposed plans to do this. In Geneva, representatives of the U.S., Great Britain, and the Soviet Union met almost continuously from 1958 through 1961. No agreement was reached, though the three nations stopped atmospheric testing for a time. Then, in August 1961, the USSR carried out a dramatic test. The U.S. resumed testing within two weeks.

There was one peace-related diplomatic agreement during this period. In 1959, the United States and the USSR signed an international treaty limiting the use of Antarctica to peaceful purposes and preventing it from becoming "the scene or object of international discord." The Antarctic Treaty is enforced by a system of international inspections at the various national bases on the continent and has been observed by all parties without incident. In fact, it has been strengthened over the years.[2,3]

THE 1960s—
CRISIS AND CONTROL

The year was 1962. The month was October. The newscasts and front pages were grim. A year earlier, the Soviet Union had suddenly resumed weapons testing. Now U.S. intelligence photographs showed that the USSR had put nuclear missiles in its Western Hemisphere outpost, Fidel Castro's Cuba. And they were pointed at the United States. The unthinkable seemed about to happen. Robert McNamara, who was President Kennedy's secretary of defense, had said he wasn't sure he would live to see the next week.

Parents and children had long, somber talks about what to do in case of nuclear attack. Bumper stickers appeared, saying, "Don't worry. They're still 90 miles away."

President Kennedy demanded that the Soviet Union remove its missiles or face nuclear war. He also placed a naval blockade around Cuba to keep Soviet ships from bringing reinforcements.

The demand worked. A few tense days later, the missiles were gone. As some Americans put it, "The Soviets blinked." The Cuban Missile Crisis marked the high point of the Cold War and the low point of the relationship between the U.S. and

*A Soviet ship carries eight canvas-
covered missiles, visible on its deck,
away from Cuba in 1962. President
Kennedy had demanded their removal.*

USSR. But the confrontation was the springboard for the first successful negotiations on nuclear weapons.

The first agreement after the Cuban Missile Crisis was the creation in 1963 of the Washington-Moscow "hot line" for use during a nuclear crisis. This direct communications link has operated ever since. It has also been used in nonnuclear situations, including the Arab-Israeli wars of 1967 and 1973.

Finally, in August 1963, the United States, Soviet Union, and United Kingdom signed the Partial Test Ban Treaty. They agreed not to conduct nuclear tests or peaceful nuclear explosions in the atmosphere, underwater, in outer space, or anywhere else if the fallout would go beyond the boundaries of the country performing the detonation. The treaty has since been signed by over 100 countries. But it has not been approved by two major nuclear powers, France and China.

Two other arms control treaties were negotiated in the late 1960s. The Outer Space Treaty, signed in 1967, was modeled on the Antarctic Treaty. It prohibits using the moon, any other celestial body, or an orbiting satellite for nuclear weapons or other weapons of mass destruction. It also limits the moon and other celestial bodies to nonmilitary uses.

The other successful negotiation in 1967 was the first treaty signed by the United States to limit the use of nuclear weapons—the Latin American Nuclear-Free Zone Treaty. It states that nuclear energy is to be used only for peaceful purposes in Mexico, Central and South America, and the Caribbean. It was designed to improve U.S. security by preventing another Cuban Missile Crisis. Cuba, however, did not ratify it. And the U.S. excludes Puerto Rico, the Virgin Islands, and the Guantanamo, Cuba, naval base. The treaty is enforced by inspections under a regional organization and the acceptance of International Atomic Energy Agency (IAEA) safeguards. The U.S. and the USSR have signed parts of the treaty but not all of it.[2,3]

THE LATE 1960s AND 1970s—NON-PROLIFERATION AND LIMITATION

Proliferation of Nuclear Weapons

Since 1945, any nation claiming to be a great power has felt compelled to develop nuclear weapons. This increase in nuclear nations is called *proliferation*. How did it happen?

Science, engineering, and technology are international. Specialists learn the same facts in school and exchange ideas around the world. In the years following World War II, nuclear energy was studied everywhere.

The U.S. took the lead in promoting its nonmilitary use. "Atoms for Peace" was part of President Eisenhower's domestic and foreign policy during the 1950s. We provided money, equipment, and training to friendly countries and those we wanted to become our allies—European nations, Japan, Israel, and Third World countries like India, Iran, and Pakistan. Out of this effort came many uses of radioactive isotopes in medicine and industry. But the technology the U.S. promoted most was the development of nuclear reactors to generate electricity.

Nuclear scientists believed this was a cheap, safe, and clean method of supplying electricity in developing countries as well as in the industrial world. And American companies were eager to sell power reactors to governments, utilities, and universities, along with the fuel to operate them.

The U.S. planned to be the only source of fissionable material. This way, it would spread the benefits of nuclear energy but not its potential for war. We strongly supported the formation of the IAEA, a UN organization, to help make this happen.

But this effort set the stage for proliferation. One of the by-products of power generation is plutonium, which could be used in weapons. Even reactors designed for research could produce plutonium. It became obvious that any country with a nuclear reactor could develop nuclear weapons.

Britain built its nuclear weapons using a combination of knowledge obtained during World War II and its own research. At the same time, China and France were operating full-scale nuclear weapons programs. Through their own efforts, they had become the fourth and fifth nuclear nations.

By the late 1960s, both the U.S. and the USSR—now called superpowers—saw the dangers of proliferation and the need to slow it down. This led to a relaxation in tensions, called "detente" (pronounced *day-tahnt*). President Nixon went to Moscow in 1972, and the two countries exchanged art exhibits, ballet troupes, and other examples of culture.

Detente led to several diplomatic agreements. The Non-proliferation Treaty, completed in 1968, was signed by the U.S., the USSR, the United Kingdom, and many other countries. France and China did not sign. It has four provisions: preventing the spread of nuclear weapons to other nations and groups; assuring that peaceful nuclear activities will not be diverted to military uses; promoting the peaceful use of nuclear power; and pursuing arms control and disarmament. The treaty appointed the IAEA as the international watchdog (to provide safeguards) over the manufacturing, shipment, and use of nuclear fuel to assure that their purpose remained peaceful.

Making War Less Likely

Several other treaties were signed during detente. The Seabed Arms Control Treaty of 1971, signed by the U.S., the USSR, and 100 other nations, is similar to the Antarctic and Outer Space treaties but is complicated by nations' differing claims to territorial waters and the ocean floor. It prohibits nuclear and other weapons of mass destruction from the seabed more than twelve miles beyond a nation's coastline.

The year 1971 also brought the Agreement to Lessen the Risk of Nuclear War between the U.S. and the Soviet Union. To keep nuclear war from breaking out, the two nations agreed to improve their efforts against accidental or unauthorized use of nuclear weapons. They also agreed to notify each other if such an accident occurs or might occur and also if any missiles might go beyond the launching country's borders.

Limiting Strategic Arms

The two countries even negotiated two treaties to limit long-range (strategic) weapons during the Strategic Arms Limitation Talks (SALT I) of 1972. The treaties' effectiveness depends on verification—the ability of each side to be sure that the other nation is living up to its agreements.

The first was the Antiballistic Missile (ABM) Treaty of 1972. The two countries agreed to limit weapons designed to protect against ballistic missiles. It was expected to curb substantially the arms race by limiting strategic missiles used for defensive purposes. This would decrease the risk of nuclear war. It limited each nation to two defensive (ABM) systems, one to protect its capital and one to protect a missile launch site. Two years later, this was changed to one system each.

The second was the Interim Agreement. It stated that for a five-year period the two countries would freeze the numbers of certain missile launchers or increase them only by destroying an equal number of older launchers. Both land-based and submarine-based missiles were included. Mobile land-based missiles were excluded.

Detente Disappears

Detente and treaty making didn't slow the arms race. Many people even feared that cultural exchanges and treaties would give the U.S. a false sense of security. They thought the USSR would take advantage of this by preparing to attack or continuing to expand into the Third World. They believed the U.S. needed to concentrate on building up its military strength.

Two other treaties were negotiated before detente evaporated. The Threshold Test Ban Treaty of 1974 went beyond the Partial Test Ban Treaty of 1963 by forbidding underground testing of weapons whose explosive force is greater than 150 kilotons (0.15 MT). As the U.S. Arms Control and Disarmament Agency says, the treaty introduces mutual restraint in limiting the power of new weapons to be tested. This treaty was not ratified by the U.S. Senate, but both countries have agreed to abide by it.

The Peaceful Nuclear Explosives Treaty of 1976 was a spin-off from the Threshold Test Ban Treaty, since the same technology is used for underground testing and for peaceful nuclear explosions (such as dam building). For this treaty also the maximum explosive force is 150 kilotons (0.15 MT). The treaty covers all underground explosions taking place away from designated nuclear weapons test sites. It, too, is unratified.[2-4]

THE 1980s—TENSION AND THE BEGINNINGS OF TRUST

Even as detente was ending, the U.S. and USSR continued to explore further limits to strategic arms. The Strategic Arms Limitation Talks (SALT II) of 1979 were intended to replace the SALT I Interim Agreement. The long-term agreement limited many kinds of strategic offensive weapons. The treaty set maximum limits for the number of launch-based multiple-warhead (MIRVed) ballistic missiles, heavy bombers with long-range cruise missiles, MIRVed missile launchers, and MIRVed ICBMs. It also banned additional numbers or types of several missile systems. It provided for procedures to assure that both sides were living up to the agreement (verification).

The SALT II accord never reached the Senate floor for ratification, because President Carter withdrew his support for the treaty after the December 1979 invasion of Afghanistan by Soviet troops. The U.S. abided by its provisions until 1986, however. Then President Reagan declared that the USSR was violating it, and the U.S. was therefore no longer obligated to observe it.

The Non-proliferation Treaty of 1968 declared the signers' intention to end all nuclear testing. In 1977, the U.S., the United Kingdom, and the USSR (China and France refused to take part) began negotiations to participate in what is called a comprehensive test ban. The main goals were to end all nuclear explosions for a given period of time. Detection equipment and inspections would provide proof that each country was living up to the agreement. These talks took place at the same time as SALT II but were even more controversial. Ronald Reagan opposed a test ban, as did the Joint Chiefs of Staff. After President Reagan took office in 1981, the subject was dropped.

By 1980, detente was dead. That year, the USSR invaded Afghanistan. The U.S. protested by withdrawing from the Summer Olympics, held in Moscow. When President Reagan took office, he began a big military expansion to regain what he considered our lost military superiority. Hostility between the superpowers increased. In reaction, many Americans became actively involved in a campaign to end the arms race.

Several influences encouraged the two countries to negotiate one arms reduction treaty and begin planning another. Some people credit our increased military strength. Others say it was the disarmament protests. There were additional ingredients. Our West European allies became inter-

*President Reagan and General Secretary
Gorbachev signing the Intermediate-Range
Nuclear Forces (INF) treaty in 1987.
The treaty eliminated several classes
of shorter- and medium-range missiles.*

ested in reducing military forces on their continent. There was growing concern in the U.S. over the size of the national budget and the national debt. Finally, the USSR under Mikhail Gorbachev appeared to be following more reasonable international policies.

The result was the Intermediate-Range Nuclear Forces (INF) Treaty of 1987, which eliminated several classes of shorter- and medium-range land-based missiles. The treaty was ratified by the U.S. Senate May 27, 1988, and went into effect shortly afterward. Since then, each country has destroyed missiles under the supervision of inspection teams from the other nation.

The success of INF has led to a renewal of cultural exchanges and a new round of talks to reduce strategic arms (the START talks). Will these positive results continue? Or will this be another short-term break in the cycle of hostility and relaxation? And most frightening of all, could we still have a nuclear war? None of the important issues have yet been resolved.[2,5-7]

FOUR

PROLIFERATION AND
THE CHANCE OF WAR

PROLIFERATION

In 1945, only one country had nuclear weapons—
the United States. In 1990, nine countries are
known or suspected nuclear powers.[1] Another
dozen or so have the technology and ability. Table
2, page 68, gives the current lineup.

Who's next? Almost anyone! Information about
producing nuclear weapons, even small and inex-
pensive ones, is easy to get. This means that almost
any country, terrorist organization, or individual
could also become a "nuclear power." The result?
Preventing nuclear war between the U.S and the
USSR doesn't mean preventing nuclear war
throughout the world.

The Non-proliferation Treaty of 1968 hasn't
been completely successful. Failure was probably
built into it. For one thing, the IAEA was given the
authority to inspect nuclear sites, but it didn't get
the power to enforce compliance with international
agreements. Five hundred nuclear facilities, over
90 percent of the total, allow IAEA inspections and
abide by them. But some nuclear nations do not—

TABLE 2
THE WORLD'S NUCLEAR POWERS

Known
All five permanent members of the UN
Security Council
    United States (1945)
    USSR (1949)
    United Kingdom (1952)
    France (1960)
    China (1964)
India (1974)

Presumed
Israel (1970)
Pakistan (mid-1980s)
South Africa (mid-1980s)

Likely in the Near Future
Argentina
Brazil
Libya

Only a Matter of Time
Iran
Iraq
Syria
Taiwan

Could But Don't Want To
Canada
Japan
Nonnuclear members of the
    European Community (EC)

Nuclear-free Zone
New Zealand

Brazil, Israel, India, Pakistan, and South Africa. Countries that have resisted signing the Non-proliferation Treaty include India, Israel, Libya, Pakistan, and South Africa.

There are other reasons why nonproliferation hasn't worked. As chapter 3 showed, nuclear technology is widespread. The basic materials— uranium and heavy water—are too easy to get through normal world trade or the black market (illegally). And it's too easy to convert power and research reactors for plutonium production.

The Reactor-Weapons Connection

Most U.S.-designed nuclear power reactors require what is called "enriched uranium" fuel. This means that the fuel contains added amounts of U-235 to make it generate power more efficiently. Enrichment is expensive. It's done commercially in the U.S. and a few other countries. In the U.S., fuel is enriched only by the DOE. This makes it relatively easy to keep track of the fuel produced and where it goes. Its purchasers are mostly electric utilities in the U.S. and abroad—all planning to be in business for a long time. So they willingly agree to restrictions.

Even so, this fuel can become the basis for nuclear weapons. As the fuel is used, the by-products make the fission process less efficient. When it's no longer economical, the fuel must be replaced. But it's often valuable enough to be reprocessed (recycled). This involves separating the plutonium and other by-products from the unburned uranium.

The nuclear industry is international. Reactor fuel may be enriched in the U.S., used in Japan, and reprocessed in Europe. The U.S. government keeps track of fuel that originates here by requiring notification each time it's moved. But a fuel shipment could be a good target for hijacking or diversion. Also, each time the fuel is reprocessed, the world's supply of plutonium grows. The more plutonium available, the greater the chance some of it will end up in a weapon belonging to a nation, government in exile, guerrilla organization, or terrorist group.

This isn't the whole story. Some commercial and research reactors use natural, not enriched, uranium fuel. Natural uranium is much easier and cheaper to produce or obtain. This makes it attractive to smaller or developing countries. Natural uranium reactors can also be used to create plutonium for weapons. According to one estimate, by the late 1990s enough plutonium will be separated each year to make over 1,200 bombs.

The Importance of Heavy Water

For most nuclear reactors to work, the neutrons that cause fission must move more slowly than they do for a weapon. So the reactors contain a "moderator" that slows neutrons to the proper speed. When the fuel is enriched uranium, the moderator is usually ordinary water.

Unfortunately, water captures neutrons as well as slowing them down. The neutron loss doesn't keep enriched uranium fuel from working efficiently. But it does with natural uranium. What this fuel needs is a good moderator that also leaves more available neutrons. A variation of water called deuterium oxide does both these jobs.

Most water (composed of hydrogen and oxygen) contains ordinary hydrogen. But some water atoms contain the hydrogen isotope called deuterium instead. Since deuterium weighs twice as much as ordinary hydrogen, the fluid is often called "heavy water."

Heavy water is rare in nature. But it is manufactured in Norway and a few other places. Heavy water is subject to IAEA controls. But it isn't hard to buy, then resell, so the manufacturer doesn't know who ends up with it. Two Norwegian shipments in 1988 were diverted this way. Both shipments were probably resold on the black market.

Even when heavy water stays with the original buyer, its use can't always be controlled. In 1959, Norway sold a supply to Israel for peaceful purposes. Ever since, Norway has been unsuccessfully attempting to inspect the reactor to make sure of this. Most experts believe Israel has actually been using the reactor to make plutonium for weapons.[2-4]

Delivery Systems

The final component needed to make a nuclear weapon is a delivery system. Today's technology allows weapons to be very small, even portable. This means they could be dropped or fired from planes or launched from the ground or the sea. If they're small enough, they can be carried in a car or backpack, making them as movable as dynamite or a plastic explosive.

Many existing military missiles can carry either conventional or nuclear weapons. They are easily bought on the international weapons market. Because of this nuclear potential, in 1987 the U.S. and six major allies—Canada, France, Italy, Japan, the United Kingdom, and West Germany—agreed to cut back on the sale of missiles or components that can fly more than about 190 miles. This has slowed the spread of missiles but not stopped it.

According to a 1989 study, twenty-four nations, mostly in the Third World, are developing or purchasing ballistic missiles. China may produce an ICBM by the year 2000. India is known to have developed a missile with a 1,500-mile range. Other nuclear nations with an interest in missiles are: Argentina, Brazil, Iran, Iraq, Israel, Pakistan, and Syria. The chance of nuclear war increases with each sale.[5,6]

The Politics of Weapons Proliferation
• The U.S. developed nuclear weapons in response to Germany's presumed atomic bomb, and later to counter the threat of Soviet aggression.

• The USSR developed nuclear weapons to keep up with the U.S.

• France developed nuclear weapons to let it pursue policies independent of the U.S.

• China developed nuclear weapons to show it was a modern power and to counter possible threats from the USSR and the U.S.

• India developed nuclear weapons to protect itself against its neighbors, China and the USSR.

• Pakistan developed nuclear weapons to keep up with India, its regional rival.

• Israel developed nuclear weapons to give it an edge in the Middle East, where it feels outnumbered and surrounded by enemies.

• Iran and Iraq were doing the same thing until they got into a long war and decided to concentrate on poison gas instead. The war was settled in 1988, and they may resume their nuclear development. Israel destroyed Iraq's reactor in 1981, but at least part of its nuclear stockpile survived.

• South Africa is developing nuclear weapons technology, in the words of a government official, "just in case."

This dismal list is likely to get longer as countries attempt to build or acquire weapons to serve their own policies. These small-scale arms races mirror the big one involving the two superpowers. Each race poses a small but significant threat to the world's nuclear balance.[6,7]

Of course, such rivalries could also work in a positive way. For example, if South Africa signs the Non-proliferation Treaty, its principal regional rivals, such as Angola and Tanzania, might sign also. But this is unlikely unless the political climate in any region becomes less hostile. However, disarmament moves by the superpowers, indicating growing trust, could spark similar improvements regionally.

World events will probably make it impossible to prevent proliferation of nuclear weapons unless some nation makes a dramatic effort. The technologies of weapons and missile production are too widespread. The most important factor may be the actions of the major powers. If the U.S. and the USSR restrain themselves by limiting testing and weapons development, other countries may follow suit.

The use of diplomacy and UN peacekeeping forces to settle disputes may also lower the level of hostility. This could lessen the "need" for nuclear weapons. However, there is no proof that this has ever happened.

A practical first step would give the IAEA more authority. It could then make complete inspections and act when it finds civilian reactors or materials being used for military purposes. At the same time, commercial nuclear nations could cooperate more closely to guard fuel shipments and reprocessing. Neither step is under way, however.

HOW NUCLEAR WAR COULD START

The chance of war exists as long as there are nuclear weapons and rivalries. With nuclear weapons in the hands of so many nations, the possibilities for starting a war are almost endless.[8] Several scenarios (scripts) for nuclear war have been written by scientists, foreign policy experts, and defense analysts. The countries involved in these fictional wars are different in each scenario, but they have many common elements:

• One superpower has enough weapons to take unusual risks. This happened in 1962, when the Soviet Union stationed missiles in Cuba (the Cuban Missile Crisis).
• The war begins in an area where the two superpowers support rival nations. Possibilities are India-Pakistan-Afghanistan, El Salvador-Nicaragua, the Middle East, southern Africa, North and South Korea, and West and East Germany. (Or the superpowers choose sides after the conflict starts.)
• There is political instability in a foreign nation. The leader wants a quick conquest to strengthen his/her power at home.
• A war starts with conventional weapons, then escalates to tactical nuclear weapons. If Iran and Iraq had already developed nuclear weapons, they might have used them instead of gas warfare during their 1980s war.

• Each superpower misjudges the other's commitment to its ally in an area.
• The egos of national leaders become involved, and no one wants to back down. This is how the U.S. got stuck in Vietnam and the USSR in Afghanistan.
• Someone in a command position misunderstands instructions and overreacts.
• Equipment malfunctions. NORAD (North American Air Defense Command) controls U.S. military communications and surveillance. It has reportedly had many instances of inaccurate radar and computer mistakes, giving false alarms of Soviet nuclear attacks.
• Someone under the stress of battle misreads weapons tracking signals. This happened in 1988. The crew of a U.S. ship in the Persian Gulf, the *Vincennes*, mistakenly thought it was being attacked by an Iranian or Iraqi airplane. The ship shot the plane down with conventional missiles, killing all on board. The plane was actually a commercial airliner on a normal civilian route and was flying away from the *Vincennes*.
• One superpower adopts the policy of launching nuclear weapons as soon as it receives a signal that the other has launched its weapons. The U.S. reportedly was planning to adopt such a "launch on warning" policy during the 1980s.
• The superpower thinks it is about to be attacked and launches its offensive weapons first. The other side retaliates.

As you see, any number can play. But the U.S. and USSR are the nations with the best opportunities to keep this from happening.

FIVE

PROTECTING
THE UNITED STATES

The United States must make vital decisions about
our own defense policies during the 1990s. We may
rethink our economic priorities. Hunger, education,
and health care are all competing for tax dollars.

Some of the questions these decisions will answer are: How much defense do we need? How
much can we afford? How much is too much?

DEFENSE SPENDING

The U.S. defense establishment is huge. The total
defense budget in 1989 was almost $300 billion. We
have over 2 million military people on active duty
at over 1,000 military bases in the U.S. and around
the world. We maintain over 350,000 military people in Europe alone. The U.S.'s total NATO-related
spending is $125 billion a year.[1,2]

Between 1981 and 1988 the U.S. spent almost
$2 trillion on defense. That comes to $750 million
a day, or $9,000 a second. According to one source,
just the arms race costs $2,000 a second, or $168
million a day, or about $61 billion a year.

Actually, military spending as a proportion of our gross national product (GNP, all we produce) has gone down since the 1960s. But it has grown 400 percent in dollar amounts.

The amounts of money devoted to defense are so large that they play a major role in the total U.S. economy. Defense policy shapes our economic priorities and limits what we spend in other areas.

Who Sets Policy?

No one person determines defense policy—not even the president. Defense policy is set mainly by what is called the "Iron Triangle," the three groups of people with the most influence over defense money and priorities:

- Government officials in the Department of Defense (DOD) and military officers at the Pentagon.
- Defense contractors—the companies that supply the military with weapons and other equipment.
- Congressional members and committees, especially those directly involved with defense issues and appropriations. It also includes senators and representatives whose districts have defense industries or military bases.

The same people often move from group to group. Military officers and members of Congress retire and go to work in the defense industry. Congressional staff members take better-paying jobs in industry. Or industry executives become officials in the DOD. There is also a government agency that works to slow the arms race, the Arms Control and Disarmament Agency. But it has little influence in setting defense policy.

Defense Policy and Civilian Priorities

The U.S. economy appears headed for trouble in the 1990s. Industrial jobs are declining, and we spend more on foreign products, like cars and stereos, than other countries buy here. Economists believe that spending more on research and development (R & D) will lead to more jobs and new products to sell abroad—something we haven't done enough of in recent years.

One of the reasons is that we spend much more of our R & D money on military items than most other countries do. According to one study, over one-third of all U.S. R & D money goes into defense. The results of defense research can't be plowed back into new production and modern equipment. This also means that priorities for new technology and products are set by the military's needs, not society's—computers, for example. The military also decides which information can be released to the civilian world.

Some commercial products do result from military spending, but they probably don't justify the original military cost. Often the military technology is untested (because it's not possible to do so except in actual war), so success of commercial spin-offs is even more risky than products developed from civilian R & D.

Dollar for dollar, military spending creates fewer jobs than civilian spending, some analysts believe. One estimate is that for every 1 percent of military spending in the GNP, economic growth is reduced by 0.5 percent. Of course, there are other ways to measure the value of money spent on defense. As you have seen, a nuclear war would destroy our lives, health, and economy. On the other hand, as former defense secretary Caspar Weinberger, a supporter of deterrence, has said, it has given us the ability to defend the nation and to back up our foreign policy.

Paying for Defense
Part of the reason defense costs so much is the way we pay for it. Military spending is different from civilian spending. For one thing, equipment is very expensive because it must meet military requirements. Also, there is only one market—the DOD—rather than a competitive marketplace. Companies are supposed to compete for defense contracts, although this is often not the case. Many large contracts are given to companies that the DOD has worked with in the past, companies that are part of the Iron Triangle.

Once the DOD selects a manufacturer, it signs a contract guaranteeing it will pay the development and production costs, plus an amount for the company's profit. This gives the company the opportunity to charge many unusual costs to the government rather than take them out of its profits. Not all companies do this, but it happens often enough. Keeping costs under control requires close regulation of the spending. But regulating long-time partners is hard to do.

The defense industry does, of course, create jobs. Senators and representatives from industrial districts find it hard to regulate defense companies, because if they closed down, voters would be left unemployed.

OFFENSIVE OR
DEFENSIVE WEAPONS?

Can the U.S. protect its security better with offensive (strategic) weapons or defensive ones?[3] For the past forty years, the answer has been offensive weapons, even though the U.S. has always stated that they are only for defense. In the 1990s, the U.S. can build a new class of strategic weapons. It could also have a large-scale defensive system. Either one will be expensive, and either could upset the nuclear balance.

NEW OFFENSIVE WEAPONS

Does the U.S. need new offensive weapons? Several strategic systems have been under development. They include the MX and the Midgetman mobile missiles and the B-2, or "Stealth," bomber.

Mobile Missiles
Missiles that can be moved from place to place have several advantages over those stationed in underground silos. They allow a more flexible response to military needs. They are also less of a target. The MX and the Midgetman mobile systems are being considered as possible replacements for the Minuteman ICBMs now in silos.[4]

The MX is a large MIRVed missile that has been under development since the 1970s. It was originally designed to be stationed on twenty-mile-

The MX Peacekeeper is a large multiple independently targetable reentry vehicle (MIRV) missile. There has been considerable controversy over how to station the MX. The present plan supports mobile basing.

long tracks and periodically moved from one pre-set location to another. A later idea was to place the missiles in silos. The present plan calls for mobile siting of the fifty existing missiles (ten warheads each), this time on railroad cars. The fifty MXs have cost an estimated $10 billion.

Why might we need the MX? People who favor military superiority believed that SALT I allowed the USSR to have too many large ICBMs. The MX would give the U.S. the ability to destroy Soviet missile sites. Some believe it's not needed because the U.S. already is superior in total weapons systems. Others oppose the MX because it will continue the arms race. They think its existence will encourage the USSR to adopt a launch-on-warning strategy, increasing the chance of a nuclear war.

The Midgetman is a much smaller mobile missile, carrying one or two warheads. Its development began after the administration and Congress failed to agree on building a fleet of MXs. Midgetman missiles would be based at military installations and moved around on special trucks.

The Midgetman would be less of a target for incoming missiles than the MX because only one or two warheads could be destroyed at a time. The Midgetman could also be more difficult to verify for arms reduction purposes, because it could be easier to conceal. The Midgetman could be the better choice to preserve the nuclear balance, some supporters of arms control say, because it cannot be considered a "first strike" weapon.

The missile is still under development. Its first test, in 1989, was a failure. Cost estimates for 500 Midgetman warheads range from $20 billion to $50 billion.

B-2 (Stealth) Bomber

This long-range airplane is designed so it doesn't register on radar screens and can slip through Soviet defense systems.[5,6] If it works, it could be used for first strikes, upsetting the nuclear balance and increasing the risk of war. Many scientists, however, do not believe Stealth will work. It is also very expensive. Each plane would cost at least $500 million. As of 1989, just one model has been built. Should the Stealth bomber be produced? It will have to compete with other new systems for money and a place in our defense strategy.

SDI—DEFENSIVE TECHNOLOGY AS THE WAY TO DISARMAMENT

Wouldn't the U.S. really be better off with a weapons system that protected the population instead of assuring its annihilation, a purely defensive system to destroy hostile nuclear weapons before they struck the U.S.? With such a system in place, wouldn't we have much less need for an offensive arsenal? The idea sounds extremely reasonable. In fact, it's the most controversial nuclear issue in decades.

The idea of a defensive system to replace MAD has been around for a long time. The U.S. and the USSR recognized this when they signed the Antiballistic Missile (ABM) Treaty in 1972. At that time, the system itself used missiles.

When Ronald Reagan became president in 1981, the idea was reborn, but without being based on missiles.[7-13] The key was a system invented by Dr. Edward Teller (usually called "the father of the H-bomb") and other scientists at Lawrence Liver-

The B-2 (Stealth) bomber is designed to elude enemy radar, possibly enabling it to mount a "first strike."

A "Star Wars" scenario: two satellites (top)
communicate while one tracks warheads
coming from the right. From left,
interceptors are launched from the ground
to hit and demolish the warheads.

more Laboratory: a new kind of space-based laser to destroy incoming nuclear missiles before they reached the U.S. This laser wouldn't be the usual focused beam of light, but a focused X-ray beam, generated by fission explosions. The system relied on computers, sensing satellites, and other new technology to be successful. But it was only an idea. No equipment existed yet.

In 1983, President Reagan announced a new program to develop a high-technology, space-based defensive shield, called the Strategic Defense Initiative, or SDI. Most people call it "Star Wars."

How the SDI Would Work

First, the system must be able to detect, identify, locate, track, and destroy incoming MIRV missiles. This must be possible during any part of the thirty minutes between the launch of the enemy missiles to the fall of the individual warheads toward their targets. Second, the defensive system must be invulnerable itself. It has to withstand nuclear explosions, heat, and the electromagnetic pulse. After almost a decade of development, SDI is still controversial. The major questions about it haven't been answered: Will it be cost-effective? Can it work? What will our allies think about it? How will it affect the peace process?

Since it began in 1983, the SDI has cost over $17 billion and used more than 10 percent of all defense-related research money. Cost could reach $1 trillion. It now appears, however, that development could take longer than planned.

Most scientists, including the eminent theoretical physicist Dr. Hans Bethe at Cornell University, say that the system as a whole cannot function as required. They believe the claims for the X-ray laser are exaggerated and it may never work. By the late 1980s, government specialists were admitting that some parts of SDI could not be ready for many years, at best.

Computers will be vital to Star Wars operations. They must control everything from sensing missiles and locating incoming warheads to firing the defensive weapons, all within a few minutes. But the computers of the 1990s may not be advanced enough for the requirements. A 1988 report by the Congressional Office of Technology Assessment predicted that the software could fail in an actual war.

Opponents also say that even if the technology were possible, the system must be 99 percent reliable to be effective. Most military systems aren't even 90 percent effective. And the Soviets could get around SDI in several ways—change rocket characteristics, add protective systems to the missiles, disable or destroy the SDI systems in space, and launch decoy missiles to divert the SDI weapons.

Supporters of SDI, on the other hand, still believe scientists can make SDI work.

Many thoughtful European experts believe that Star Wars will actually increase the danger of war by shifting the military emphasis to conventional weapons. This could mean a greater risk of war on European land. As in other limited wars, the superpowers themselves would be far from the conflict.

HOW SDI AFFECTS THE PEACE PROCESS

Opponents also say SDI is destabilizing. It can be used to improve our first-strike capability, then defend against any possible retaliation. For instance, it could be used to destroy Soviet surveillance satellites.

It was the fear of this that led to the ABM Treaty of 1972. Opponents believe testing or deploying SDI violates not only the ABM Treaty but the Outer Space Treaty and SALT I. The Outer Space Treaty forbids the orbiting of "objects carrying nuclear weapons" or the stationing of such weapons there "in any manner whatsoever." SALT I forbids the development, testing, and deploying of space-based offensive missiles. Opponents also think SDI's automated decision making increases the chance of war.

SDI supporters say that the Soviets never really believed in the ABM treaty. They think Americans are foolish to believe that the Soviets would choose a piece of paper over technology. The U.S. shouldn't depend on diplomacy, either. SDI will add to our deterrent strength, they believe. Opponents— including scientists, diplomats, and clergy—say reliance on technology means a wide-open arms race. For one thing, the Soviet Union could build an identical system, then use it to destroy SDI in space.

The U.S. says the space-based system is not offensive for the purposes of arms reduction talks. But so far the Soviets are calling SDI an offensive system that must be included in any negotiations. They have even stated that they won't limit offensive weapons if the U.S. builds SDI. In fact, one Soviet official has said it will disrupt the nuclear balance and make nuclear war more likely.

Right now, the U.S. wants to test components in space. Will this violate the ABM treaty? Experts who oppose SDI think so, and so do several government officials. Lt. Gen. George Monahan, head of the Strategic Defense Initiative Organization, which is in charge of Star Wars development, has told Congress that tests planned for the mid-1990s would be violations. Secretary of Defense Dick Cheney says that having SDI is worth withdrawing from the treaty.

While the debate continues over the feasibility of SDI's "impermeable shield," what are the prospects for reducing existing nuclear arsenals?

SIX

REDUCING THE
NUCLEAR ARSENALS

CAN WE TRUST THE SOVIETS?

Many experts believe that the Cold War is over. One is George Kennan, a diplomat and Cold War analyst for forty years. Kennan developed the idea of containment or deterrence, and has long advocated a realistic view of U.S.-Soviet relations. In 1989, he asked the United States to take a new look at attitudes toward the USSR and our level of nuclear and conventional weapons. Kennan made these points:

- Our nuclear and conventional strength is far beyond what we need to protect our interests.
- Our military strength creates mistrust.
- It diverts resources that could be used better in other ways.
- We exaggerate the strength and numbers of Warsaw Pact forces.
- We should consider Soviet intentions and policies, not just its maximum military strength.[1]

Former president Richard Nixon has said there are new opportunities to negotiate for better U.S.-USSR relations, but the U.S. must do it by offering specific choices so that hostilities will be reduced on our terms.[2] In the post–Cold War era, the U.S. can take many steps to reduce the possibility of nuclear war. The USSR has already taken some on its own. It is reducing both weapon and conventional strength in Eastern Europe as part of a general military reduction.

What the Soviets Think
People in the Soviet Union see the world differently than we do. They see their nation surrounded by enemies, in Europe and Asia. For a long time the USSR has been the largest country on earth in area. But it hasn't always been powerful.

In fact, in the 1930s it was so weak that it signed a peace pact with Hitler's Germany to avoid war with this stronger power. When Hitler's armies invaded the Soviet Union anyway, they almost defeated it. Land battles killed millions of Russian soldiers, while starvation in Leningrad and other cities killed millions of civilians. In all, the USSR lost about 20 million people in World War II.

In the end, the bitter cold Russian winters, the courage of the people, and American supplies defeated the Germans on the "Eastern front." As the war ended, the Soviet leaders vowed their country would never be weak and vulnerable again. The first step was to surround themselves with friendly countries, like Poland, Czechoslovakia, and China, or neutral ones, like Finland and Austria. They turned the portion of Germany they occupied into the Communist state of East Germany. When China became unfriendly, they stationed a large armed force along the Soviet-Chinese border. After the U.S. and its allies formed NATO (the North Atlantic Treaty Organization) to defend Western Europe from Soviet aggression, the USSR formed the Warsaw Pact with its Eastern European allies.

The USSR improved its nuclear arsenal to match or surpass the U.S.'s weapons supply. It also greatly expanded its arsenal of tanks and other land-based weapons systems to protect itself and its allies against possible aggression by NATO.

What We Think

Americans think about the world from our own point of view. This includes the arms race. Our policy assumes the Soviet Union will be the aggressor in a confrontation. We think of our troops and weapons in Europe and around the world as defensive.[3–9]

In the 1990s as in the past, there are three widely held points of view: (1) military superiority, (2) deterrence, and (3) diplomatic negotiations.

Superiority: Do We Still Need It?

Many respected experts say Yes. The Soviet Union has a worldwide navy and air force. It has combat forces in countries bordering the West or Western allies in Europe, Asia, and the Middle East, and military and security advisers in the Middle East, Africa, Asia, and Latin America. It has also financed and assisted advisory roles by its allies in various regions of the world. An example is Cuba's role in the affairs of Angola and Ethiopia.

Supporters of U.S. military superiority also point out that the Soviet Union particularly wants to expand its influence and dominance in the Third

World. It supplies many billions of dollars' worth of military equipment abroad every year.

Cuba is the Soviet Union's most important Third World ally, receiving half of all Soviet foreign-aid funds. Cuba and the USSR have been the main supporters of the Sandinistas in Nicaragua. This shows the Soviet Union's interest in expanding its influence in Latin America and the Caribbean, where the United States has a traditional interest.

The Soviet Union has a much bigger military structure than the United States does—through R & D programs and the purchase and theft of Western technology. The U.S. must build up its strategic nuclear forces. We also need new systems of "enhanced deterrence," such as the Strategic Defense Initiative (SDI).

In fact, people who believe in military superiority say it was only the U.S.'s greater strength that forced the USSR to agree to the INF Treaty. President Reagan believed this during his terms in office. But further buildups are being resisted in both countries because of budget deficits and social and economic needs.

Is Deterrence an Adequate Policy?

Proponents of deterrence don't necessarily object to all the military development favored by believers in superiority. But they ask, "In the nuclear age, what is military superiority?"

The traditional way of calculating superiority is by the number of weapons. That's all right for conventional wars, they say. But having more nuclear weapons doesn't mean that we can win. In fact, the bigger the arsenal, the less secure we become.

In a nuclear war, everyone loses equally. So

instead of being a win-lose situation, it's really a lose-lose situation. If you attack first, you automatically destroy yourself. In fact, the arms race has made the U.S. and USSR hostages to each other. The best we can do under these conditions is to achieve stability by linking the security of the two countries.

Can Negotiations Work?

In the 1990s, the U.S. and the USSR are again reducing hostilities and negotiating to create a more secure world future. The INF Treaty is an example. In the late 1970s, both nations were developing new weapons systems. The USSR had a new class of intermediate-range weapons called SS-20s. In the mid-1980s, the U.S. responded with its own new intermediate-range weapons called Pershing II and cruise missiles, which we installed in Europe. The USSR believed that the Pershing missiles would upset the weapon balance of terror and wanted them removed. To avoid this risk, both countries decided to take another risk—trying to remove weapons while maintaining the balance. The risk was worth it: the INF Treaty of 1987 gave each side what it wanted. Both the USSR's SS-20s and the U.S.'s Pershing missiles are being removed and destroyed, along with several other types.

Why were the negotiations successful? Supporters of U.S. military superiority think that it forced the Soviets to the bargaining table. Others think that the treaty reflected the reality that both nations have to reduce the amount of money they spend on defense. It also reflected the desire of many people in Europe to reduce the number of weapons stationed on their soil.

The two superpowers will probably always be

rivals. But rivalry doesn't have to include nuclear war. Negotiation could be the way to greatly reduce the chance of war and greatly improve the chance for peace. How can this be done? The answer is, step by step. Here are some of them:

- Reduce the number of nuclear weapons.
- Stop the introduction of new nuclear weapons systems.
- Emphasize defensive, not offensive, weapons.
- Stop testing nuclear weapons.
- Control the proliferation of nuclear weapons.
- Reduce the numbers and types of nonnuclear weapons. These include conventional, biological, and chemical weapons.

Each step is controversial—and scary. Each step requires the U.S. and the USSR to increase their level of trust in each other. And each step is opposed by some experts who still believe that only military superiority can prevent war.

Diplomacy is more important than it has been in many years. But successful diplomacy requires trust. One way to build trust between hostile rivals is by verification—the use of technology to prove that each side is living up to its promises.

TRUST BUT VERIFY— VERIFY, BUT TRUST

Some experts doubt that verification can work. Former Secretary of Defense Caspar Weinberger has said that verification is no substitute for compliance—living up to the letter of the treaty. Of course, compliance depends on both sides playing by the same rules. If each side judges compliance differently, any agreement will fail. Verification also depends on both sides playing by the same rules.[10]

The best verification system would be "anytime, anywhere" inspection on demand. Neither side is willing to allow that. Each has nuclear secrets it wants to protect. But both sides could probably accept limited verification that would make significant violations unlikely.

Most of the technology to verify any agreement already exists. As long ago as 1979, Secretary of Defense Harold Brown stated that the U.S. had the tools to monitor the entire Soviet nuclear weapons program—"development, testing, production, deployment [stationing], training, and operation." Here are some of these monitoring techniques:

• Satellites. For many years, we have had satellites that observe the entire earth, searching for ICBM test launches, nuclear explosions, and other weapons-related activities. A worldwide network of ground stations and ships receives information from them. Some satellites take photographs and TV pictures, while others are heat sensing or listen in on all military communications and radar-station transmissions. We put more sensitive satellites into orbit each year. (The USSR does the same thing.)

• Radar and radio. The U.S. also uses these to monitor Soviet weapons testing.

• Seismic stations. Earthquake monitoring techniques can be adapted to monitor underground weapons testing.

• Visual inspections. On-site inspection by experts can make sure that treaty provisions are being carried out.

• Dispute handling. To settle treaty disputes, in 1972 the U.S. and USSR established a joint Standing Consultative Commission. Opinions differ on how successful it has been. Some U.S. experts believe it has performed well, but others think it has failed badly.

Can verification succeed? The record for the INF Treaty of 1987 indicates that it does. The treaty contains strict verification procedures. Every step of the missiles' destruction is spelled out. Locations in the U.S., the USSR, and allied countries for on-site inspection by the other side are named. Technical experts count the numbers of missiles and launching vehicles. They watch the equipment's destruction and make sure nothing is left intact. They also do periodic surprise checks for compliance. Inspectors are stationed permanently at one assembly plant in each country. U.S. inspectors stay at the USSR's former SS-20 plant, and Soviet teams are at the old Pershing plant in Magna, Utah. The treaty also establishes a Special Verification Commission to settle any disputes.

In fact, the only limits on INF verification were included on purpose. The U.S., for example, wanted to retain the nuclear warheads rather than destroy them. Destruction would mean letting Soviet experts see how they were designed. The U.S. also insisted on wording allowing the upgrading of NATO's weapon forces. The success of verification under the INF Treaty means that it can also be used in agreements to resolve other nuclear issues, such as arms reduction, proliferation, and a total ban on weapons' testing.

These issues would be difficult enough with only the U.S. and the USSR involved. But the superpowers aren't the only nuclear powers. The list is growing all the time.

COMPREHENSIVE TEST BAN

If the world already has many times more nuclear weapons than it needs, why do we still need to test them? The U.S. evaluates new weapons systems because they provide more efficient and less expensive explosive and radiation power. Some new systems, like the neutron bomb, are tailored to fit specific military needs.

We also test the condition of existing systems, for safety and their ability to prevent unauthorized use. And we learn how long weapons systems are stable—for instance, how long tritium can remain in a weapon. Tests also have another purpose: If there is a comprehensive test ban, the U.S. wants a stockpile of reliable advanced weapons. The USSR is undoubtedly conducting similar tests for the same reasons.

What would a comprehensive test ban accomplish? It would stop both sides from introducing new weapons systems. It would also help reduce the numbers of weapons. Older, less reliable systems that were taken out of use couldn't be replaced.

If we don't test our weapons systems, won't we weaken our security? Supporters of a test ban say that doesn't have to happen. Explosive blast, heat, and electromagnetic pulse can be tested with nonnuclear materials and computer simulations. Simulations for radiation effects are also being developed.

In fact, a 1988 law requires a Nuclear Test Ban Readiness Program, which must develop other ways to evaluate weapons. However, advocates of continued testing say no substitute method is reliable. Supporters of a test ban also believe that tests of existing systems cost too much—$25 million per explosion. Routine maintenance and periodic parts replacement can provide the same level of reliability. They say a system's safety and ability to prevent unauthorized use can be proved without testing the warhead, because only the nonnuclear components are involved.[11–13]

The key to a successful test ban is verification. The U.S. would have to be assured that the USSR couldn't perform secret tests. The USSR would need the same proof. For example, one side might try to make its tests undetectable, or it might disguise them as earthquakes. Fortunately, proven verification techniques exist.

Since 1986, U.S.-USSR teams have evaluated seismic monitoring systems at the two nations' weapons test sites and nearby. The U.S. government has developed a system called CORRTEX that uses measuring devices at the test site. Other U.S. scientists have investigated a second on-site method. The USSR prefers off-site verification. Several studies, including one by the Congressional Office of Technology Assessment, say CORRTEX and the Soviet system are equally valid.

According to some experts, a seismic station far from the test site could detect a 0.1 MT explosion. An on-site station could detect one as small as 0.01 MT. Satellites that now monitor the Limited Test Ban Treaty could also verify compliance with a comprehensive test ban. Once both sides adopt a verification method, they would be in a position to ratify the Threshold Test Ban Treaty of 1974 (see pages 62–63). This could then lead to negotiations to ban all nuclear tests.

American and Soviet scientists toast each other at a test site in Nevada after conducting a nuclear test ban verification experiment.

NUCLEAR ARMS REDUCTION

The INF Treaty was a success, but it eliminated only some classes of weapons. It reduced the total number by only about 3 percent. Both sides are free to replace the destroyed weapons with others that serve the same purposes. The U.S. has already developed a new missile it wants to place in Germany. According to some experts, NATO still has about 4,600 short- and long-range nuclear weapons in Europe, even without those removed under INF. Also, the treaty didn't touch the strategic weapons at all.

When the U.S. and the USSR signed the SALT II agreements in 1979, they stated the number of strategic weapons that were subject to it.

	U.S.	USSR
Single-warhead ICBMs	1,054	1,398
MIRVed ICBMs	550	608
Single-warhead SLBMs	656	950
MIRVed SLBMs	496	144
Heavy bombers	573	156

If each MIRVed missile had 10 warheads, each side possessed about 10,000 strategic warheads. More recent unofficial estimates are (approximately):

	U.S.	USSR
ICBM warheads	2,100	6,400
SLBM warheads	5,300	2,100
Other warheads and bombs	3,400	2,400

To build on the INF success, the U.S. and the USSR are already involved in START (Strategic Arms Reduction Talks). Even if START leads to a 50 percent reduction in ICBMs, both countries will still be able to destroy each other with the other 50 percent. Meanwhile, both sides continue to develop new strategic weapons.[13-16]

A strategic arms reduction treaty may be harder to negotiate than INF, and may be more limited in scope. Strategic weapons are the heart of deterrence for both superpowers. Both need to feel confident about their ability to strike back if attacked. So any treaty will probably leave many strategic weapons alone and permit flight testing of missile systems (without warheads).

Verification will be difficult. Accurate identification and counting of existing missiles will be needed beforehand so that realistic limits can be negotiated. The same accuracy will be needed after the treaty goes into effect, to verify compliance.

If START is to succeed, it must settle several issues:

- Should the number of missiles be limited, or the number of warheads? In other words, should MIRVed weapons be allowed?
- Should land-based missiles be at stationary or mobile locations?
- How will launch sites affect the ability to accurately count the number of missiles each side has?
- Should the two sides be permitted a specified and equal number of missiles?
- What should be the role of cruise missiles?
- How will treaty provisions be verified?

MIRVed weapons are attractive because they are efficient and cost-effective. So are weapons stationed at mobile locations, such as on railroad cars. But both types make verification difficult. Mobile intermediate-range weapons were outlawed in INF. Should mobile strategic weapons be banned, too? Or, as one analyst suggests, should there be a compromise? For instance, the treaty might permit a limited number of single-warhead, mobile strategic missiles.

Supporters of deterrence have suggested that START should guarantee security of strategic systems. At the same time, it could keep the two sides from trying to outdo each other with first-strike superiority. First-strike buildups could be minimized in three ways: scaling back on the size of the buildups; protecting missiles better to make them less attractive as targets; and removing ICBMs altogether.

START negotiators are generally believed to be favoring a 30–50 percent cut in numbers of weapons, with no more than 6000 warheads for each side. Total elimination of ICBMs is probably unlikely anytime soon, say supporters of deterrence. The small, maneuverable cruise missiles may actually be more destabilizing than the larger ICBMs and SLBMs, because they are easier to defend against than ballistic missiles. Also, they may be easy to conceal using "stealth" technology that makes them invisible to radar.

Reductions in nuclear missiles with ranges under 300 miles must also be negotiated. The USSR has already removed some of these missiles from Eastern Europe. The U.S. and its NATO allies want to negotiate a partial reduction, but after both sides reduce their conventional forces.

SEVEN

PEACE, PEACE ADVOCATES, AND SOCIAL JUSTICE

The U.S. government has always believed that the nation's freedom depends on the military strength to defend it. In other words, the United States has developed the power to fight a "just" or defensive war, if necessary. Most people would put the Revolutionary War, the Civil War, World Wars I and II, and the Korean conflict in this category. Many would also put the Cold War there.

But the U.S. has waged other wars, which many people considered less just, or even unjust. In the nineteenth century, the desire to expand our borders was a big factor in the War of 1812, the Mexican War (1846–48), the Indian wars (1870s–90s), and the Spanish-American War (1898–1901). Large numbers of Americans thought those wars were wrong. The same thing happened during the Vietnam War (1960s–70s).

People who oppose war—totally or in part—have lived throughout history and on every continent. They're often called pacifists. What kind of people are they? Some, like India's Mohandas Gandhi, have been against all forms of violence or resistance, even to save their own lives. Others oppose specific wars—such as Americans who spoke and acted against the Vietnam War. Or they are against specific weapons, like poison gas used in the Iran-Iraq War of the 1980s.

Some peace advocates have reluctantly decided certain wars are "just." During the Civil War, American pacifists decided the abolition of slavery was worth fighting for. Some twentieth-century pacifists decided to oppose the evil of Hitler and the Nazis by taking part in World War II. Some are religious and some are atheists. Some work on their own, others as part of organizations. Today the U.S. has thousands of peace organizations (see pages 150–53).

Some people equate pacifism with cowardice. But being an advocate for peace takes courage. In acting contrary to majority opinion, pacifists have been called cowards and traitors. Pacifists have gone to jail and, in some cases, been killed for their beliefs.

GOING BEYOND
OPPOSITION TO WAR

For many people, *opposing war* is just the first part of this examination of themselves and society.[1] The next step is often harder—deciding to work *for peace*. Why? For one thing, war is easier to visualize than peace. War means action and equipment. We can see it in our minds' eyes and, all too often, on the evening news.

Peace, on the other hand, sounds rather passive. If peace is the absence of war, it's almost impossible to visualize. It's like visualizing a hole. The

American philosopher William James was a peace advocate. Ninety years ago he called for a "moral equivalent of war"—something that's exciting, that captures people's imaginations and makes them want to work together.

Does such a "moral equivalent" exist? Many people think it does, in the form of acting to bring about a just society. In fact, they define peace as the establishment of true justice for everyone.

People throughout history have connected peace and justice. All the major world religions make the connection. So does the most important document to come out of the United Nations, the Universal Declaration of Human Rights. The peace-justice connection was one of the main forces in the 1960s during the civil rights and antiwar struggles. And it's at work today, as people look for new social and economic priorities to preserve and improve life on earth. The more people have learned about the consequences of nuclear war, the more popular peacemaking has become.

EARLY ADVOCATES FOR PEACE

The first American pacifists were the Quakers. This Christian movement, officially called the Society of Friends, was formed in England in the mid-seventeenth century. From the beginning, Quakers have opposed war and refused to use weapons. William Penn (1644–1718), the founder of Pennsylvania, put his Quaker beliefs into practice by dealing with the Indians only on a peaceful basis. The colony originally had no army or militia. "Peace is maintained by Justice," he said. Penn was an internationalist. He proposed the establishment of a European parliament as a route to peace.

The Revolutionary War brought independence to the United States, but not peace. One of the first cabinet positions established under the Constitution was the War Department (now called the Department of Defense). The nation might also have had a Peace Department, if Congress had taken the advice given in 1793 by two patriotic scientists, Benjamin Rush (1745–1813) and Benjamin Banneker (1731–1806). Rush, a physician, was a signer of the Declaration of Independence. Banneker, a free African American, was a mathematician and the publisher of a popular almanac. They called for "an office for promoting and preserving perpetual peace in our country."

The modern peace movement began as a reaction to the early-nineteenth-century Napoleonic Wars in Europe and the War of 1812 in North America. The first organization was the New York Peace Society, formed in 1815. Peace advocates of the mid-1800s included ministers, philosophers, and antislavery activists. Two of the most famous were the writers Emerson and Thoreau. The two were friends but took quite different approaches to pacifism.

Philosopher and writer Ralph Waldo Emerson (1803–82) believed that people's love of war reflected their behavior and attitudes. In 1838 he wrote an essay called "War," observing, "We surround ourselves . . . with true images of ourselves in things," such as armies and weapons. These things "serve as an index to show where man is now; what a bad, ungoverned temper he has; what an ugly neighbor he is; how his affections halt; how low his hope lies. He who loves the bristle of bayonets only sees in their glitter what beforehand he feels in his heart."

Emerson felt that if people come to see that every person "was another self" with whom to join, like right and left hands, they would abandon the materials of war. Advocating peace does not mean passivity, Emerson said. No one "ever embraced the cause of peace" solely to be "plundered and slain." There is "an active purpose, some equal motive, some flaming love," he said. "The cause of peace is not the cause of cowardice."

Emerson's friend Henry David Thoreau (1817–62) is best known today as the author of *Walden,* a work celebrating nature and the simple life. But he was also famous as a peace activist. Thoreau opposed the Mexican War of the 1840s and refused to pay taxes to support it. For this he was arrested and spent a rather famous night in jail. Folklore says that Emerson came to visit him in jail and asked him, "David, what are you doing in there?" Thoreau supposedly snapped back, "Waldo, what are you doing out there?" Thoreau also wrote an essay called "On the Duty of Civil Disobedience" in which he told people to act on their consciences when they believe the government is wrong.[2,3]

PEACE ADVOCATES IN THE EARLY TWENTIETH CENTURY

The Nobel Peace Prize is one of several awards established in the will of Alfred Nobel (1838–96), a Swedish chemist who made a fortune from manufacturing weapons and explosives. He was the inventor of dynamite. The first Nobel Peace Prize was awarded in 1901. The 1985 Peace Prize went to the International Physicians for the Prevention of

Nuclear War, cofounded by U.S. and Soviet physicians.

Women became recognized leaders in twentieth-century peace movements. Jane Addams (1860–1935) is best known as a social reformer and cofounder of Hull House in Chicago, an early-twentieth-century social service agency for immigrants. In her day, Addams was equally prominent as a peace activist, beginning to speak for nonviolence during the Spanish-American War (1898–1901). She advocated turning war-oriented courage and sacrifice to the solution of social problems instead. After World War I began (1914), Addams tried to bring the two sides together for a peaceful settlement—an effort involving women from all the countries at war. When this failed, she tried to convince President Woodrow Wilson and congressional leaders to keep the U.S. out of the war. As pro-war sentiments grew, Addams became increasingly unpopular. But once the war was over, she again became active internationally. She served as president of the Women's International League for Peace and Freedom (which still exists), calling for a strong League of Nations. In 1931 Jane Addams was one of two recipients of the Nobel Peace Prize.

William James (1842–1910), psychologist and philosopher, took a "pragmatic" approach to pacifism. During the first decade of the twentieth century, he wrote about the need for a "moral equivalent of war." He developed the idea of mandatory national service for peaceful ends, with army-style discipline, to help solve social problems.

Despite the worldwide enthusiasm for peace, by 1914, Europe had once again become the scene of war—the worst by far in terms of soldiers and civilians killed and new, more powerful weapons. World War I saw the introduction of submarines, heavy artillery, airplanes, and poison gas. By the time the war ended in 1918, the major world powers seemed ready to take new steps toward peace.

The League of Nations was the first genuinely worldwide government organization devoted to preventing war through disarmament, international cooperation, and arbitration of disputes. The League was founded after the end of World War I, largely through the efforts of U.S. president Woodrow Wilson (1856–1924). But the U.S. never became a member. The Covenant, or charter, of the League became part of the peace treaty.

The League of Nations had no real power and failed in the 1930s because the strong nations were not committed to its purposes. However, many of its specialized agencies, such as the World Court and the International Labor Organization, still exist. The League's headquarters in Geneva, Switzerland, now serves as the European home of the United Nations.

At the same time that the great powers were fighting wars or preparing for them, one of history's greatest pacifists was showing the strength of his philosophy. India's Mohandas Gandhi (1869–1948) developed his method of passive resistance, called *satyagraha,* based on ideas taken from Hindu and Western philosophy. Gandhi used the principles of nonviolence to lead India to freedom from British rule. He believed in the unity of all people and lived according to the Hindu faith, including the concept of "ahimsa," meaning nonviolence and a respect for life based on the belief in the unity of all life. Gandhi supplemented this with Christian

President Woodrow Wilson, shown here in France in 1918. Through his efforts, the League of Nations was founded. Ironically, his own country never became a member.

and Moslem principles. He believed in satyagraha unconditionally, even to the point of not defending against attacks, either personally or nationally.

After thirty years of nonviolent resistance and fasting by growing numbers of Indians, India gained its independence after World War II. Though Gandhi believed that the country could govern itself by nonviolent means, this did not turn out to be the case.

Gandhi was assassinated in 1948 during a prayer meeting. He inspired generations of people around the world to use similar methods to achieve social goals. Even forty years after his death, he continues to serve as an inspiration for peaceful change. His method was used by Martin Luther King, Jr., and others in the civil rights movement of the 1960s and 1970s.

THE NUCLEAR AGE

World War II brought new and unimagined horrors to the world, from the Holocaust to the atomic bomb. Many nations and individuals spoke for the need to establish peace. One of these was Albert Einstein (1879–1955), the great physicist whose theory about mass and energy led to the development of nuclear power. Ironically, he was a lifelong pacifist.

Einstein, who was Jewish, came to the U.S. from Germany in the 1930s. Einstein didn't oppose World War II, because he thought Hitler was too great a menace. At the urging of other scientists, he wrote to President Roosevelt in 1939 and again in 1940 explaining that the U.S. must develop nuclear weapons before Germany did. Even so, he opposed using the bomb on Japan in 1945.

*Physicist Albert Einstein was a peace
activist who favored the international control
of nuclear energy. He once said, "You cannot
simultaneously prevent and prepare for war."*

From then until his death, Einstein publicly supported the ideas of a strong world government and international control of nuclear energy. He criticized both the U.S. and the USSR for the arms race. In his last year, he urged the world to give up nuclear weapons, including the just-developed hydrogen bomb.

The United Nations was founded in San Francisco in 1945, as World War II was coming to an end. Since then, it has served as a forum and meeting ground for diplomatic activity. Although the United Nations has not prevented the arms race, it has been effective in mediation and peacekeeping for many nonnuclear conflicts. In 1988, the UN's Peacekeeping Force was awarded the Nobel Peace Prize.

Albert Schweitzer (1875–1965) was a pacifist and humanitarian who spent decades in Africa practicing medicine. For this work, Schweitzer received the Nobel Peace Prize in 1952. He also spoke out on nuclear war, saying that the world is faced with two risky choices: to continue the "mad arms race," with the danger of war, or to abandon nuclear weapons and hope the U.S. and the USSR can find a way to live peacefully. He once said, "Those who live by the bomb will perish by the bomb."

Pope John XXIII (1881–1963), who led the Roman Catholic Church during the 1950s and early 1960s, wrote a major position paper (encyclical) called "Pacem in Terris," or "Peace on Earth." He expressed his "deep sorrow" about the "enormous stocks of armaments" made by industrial countries, which required "a vast outlay of intellectual and economic resources." He said people live in "constant fear" of the "dreadful violence" that could storm down on them, because of the arms race, through "some uncontrollable and unexpected chance." Even nuclear testing, he said, could have "fatal consequences for life on earth." Only "inner convictions" will banish fear of war and allow people to reduce nuclear weapons, let alone abolish them, he said. "Reason," not "force of arms," should govern relations between nations.

Martin Luther King, Jr. (1929–1968), a Baptist minister, made Christian nonviolent resistance the cornerstone of his campaigns for racial justice and equality in the U.S. King was also an advocate of world peace. Influenced in part by Gandhi, King believed Gandhi was the first to mold Jesus's love ethic into a tool for large-scale social change. King was not a total pacifist but believed nuclear weapons made war outdated. He opposed the Cold War, the policy of deterrence, the arms race, and the Vietnam War. King received the Nobel Peace Prize in 1964 for fighting injustice by peaceful means. He was assassinated in Memphis in 1968 while helping sanitation workers gain better pay.

What does it take to speak and act against war or in behalf of peace and justice? Today, as in the past, it takes courage, knowledge of the issues, ethical or moral inspiration, and a thoughtful decision.

People oppose nuclear war from several viewpoints:

- Medical. Nuclear war will be the last epidemic, wiping out most human life.

- Social. Preparation for nuclear war is eating up resources that could be used for improving education and health.
- Rational. It is illogical to pursue a policy that develops more than ten times the number of weapons needed to destroy all life on earth, let alone defend the U.S.
- Economic. Our military-oriented economy spends research and development monies on scientific projects that benefit the military, not the entire country.
- Personal. Nuclear war is counter to their values, ideals, and morality.

Personal values and ideals grow out of family life, education, community, and religion or ethical beliefs. They are the basis for many people's antiwar activities. Their power makes people consider what it means to be truly human—how to live a meaningful life within an equally "human" society.

JUDEO-CHRISTIAN BELIEFS CONCERNING PEACE

The long history of Christianity has had two threads concerning war and peace. One is the idea of the "just war," waged in defense of homes or principles. The other is the necessity for peace and the activity of peacemaking.

In the nuclear age, the two threads come together. Many religious leaders have reexamined the idea of a "defensive war," asking, If nuclear war means annihilation, can it ever be considered good and just? If the answer is no, peacemaking becomes the only alternative.

116

Some Christian denominations have always lived peacefully—the Friends (Quakers), Brethren, Mennonites, and Jehovah's Witnesses. Others have placed new emphasis on it in the recent past. They recognize the long tradition of peacemaking in the Bible and the statements and actions of religious people.

Today's religious peacemakers come from both "liberal" and "conservative" traditions and are found among Roman Catholics, Protestants, and Jews. Pope John Paul II (Roman Catholic), Billy Graham (conservative Baptist), and William Sloane Coffin (liberal Protestant) are a few of the most prominent.

The Roman Catholic bishops of America made strong public statements against nuclear war during the 1980s. "We do not perceive any situation in which the deliberate initiation of nuclear warfare, on however a restricted scale, can be morally justified. Nonnuclear attacks by another state must be resisted by other than nuclear means." They support a halt in the arms race and call the initiation of nuclear war "unjustifiable in any form." They have also questioned the morality of Star Wars and opposed the deployment of additional weapons systems. They have said the policy of deterrence "is not a stable long-term method of keeping the peace among sovereign states" and is acceptable only if not directed at civilian populations and in the context of arms reduction and nonproliferation efforts.[4,5]

The governing bodies of the United Methodists, the Lutheran Church of America, the United Church of Christ, the Episcopal Church, United Presbyterians, and other Protestant denominations have also spoken out against nuclear war and in favor of peace. Billy Graham has stated his renewed belief in peacemaking and the need to understand the difference between patriotism and morality. Several years ago he made a peace pilgrimage to the Soviet Union as a part of this effort. William Sloane Coffin calls for replacing the arms race with a race to disarm. And he says, "We must recognize that peace is not just the absence of conflict but the presence of justice."

THE BIBLE AND PEACE

People have quoted the Bible for many purposes, and interpretations don't always agree. But the emphasis on peace runs through both the Old and New Testaments, providing inspiration and continuity.[6]

The Bible of the Jewish religion, which Christians call the Old Testament, clearly depicts a God of justice and also one of peace. In fact, the universal symbol of peace—the dove with an olive branch in its mouth—comes from Genesis (chapters 8 and 9), in the story of Noah and the flood sent to destroy the world's evil. From the ark, Noah sent a dove out three times looking for hope that life would continue on land. The first time the dove came back with nothing. The second time it came back with the branch, showing that land existed, the symbol of hope. The third time, the dove didn't return, signaling that it had found a new life and that people could also. God reaffirmed this to Noah by sending another sign of peace and continuity—a rainbow.

Perhaps the most famous Biblical quotation on peace and war is found in Isaiah 2:4. The prophet looks forward to the time when, at God's direction, nations "shall beat their swords into plowshares, and their spears into pruning hooks; one nation shall not lift up the sword against another nation, neither shall they learn war anymore." The paragraph appears virtually word for word in the book of another prophet, Micah (4:3). Psalm 46:8–9 shows God taking direct action: "From end to end of the earth he stamps out war; he breaks the bow, he snaps the spear and burns the shield in the fire."

The New Testament is built around Jesus as the Prince of Peace. In the Beatitudes (Matthew 5:9) Jesus called peacemakers the sons of God. There are just two major rules, he said: love God and love your neighbors.

In Romans, chapter 8, the apostle Paul equates the spiritual outlook with life and peace. The apostle James (3:17–18) adds reason and justice: "the wisdom from above is . . . peace-loving, considerate, and open to reason; it is straightforward and sincere, rich in mercy and in the kindly deeds that are its fruit. True justice is the harvest reaped by peacemakers from seeds sown in a spirit of peace." On the other hand, James says (4:1–2) war results when people become greedy and try to take what they can't get legitimately.

BUDDHISM

Buddhism is the religion built on the beliefs and teachings of Siddhārtha Gautama, known as the Buddha (approximately sixth century B.C.), a social reformer who believed in the equality of all people. Its adherents are found throughout the world. Many schools or denominations of Buddhism exist, with different interpretations of the basic beliefs.

What all Buddhists share is a belief in gentleness, compassion, love of all living creatures, charity, fellowship, and hospitality. Killing is always to be avoided. A popular ethical text, the *Dhammapada*, urges people to repay evil with good. People can put these humane ideals into operation by being flexible in dealing with others, avoiding egotism and extreme positions, and practicing social cooperation.[7]

ISLAM

Islam proclaims the same God as Judaism and Christianity and shares roots with both. Though the greatest Islamic prophet of God is Mohammad, followers accept Abraham, Noah, Moses, and Jesus as great prophets. Islam is a total system of living, involving both worship and rules of conduct for everyday life.

One of the most important of these is social service—giving to the needy and taking steps to stop people's suffering. Islam's holy book, the Koran, restricts "just" war to the need to preserve religious principles and God's rules. War-making for power or worldly success is strictly forbidden.

EIGHT

TAKING A STAND

Living according to the principles of peace can be a powerful message to others. Taking a public stand against war and for peace is another message.

You can prevent nuclear war. Probably not all by yourself, of course! But if you decide to take a stand, the first step is to believe that you—as an individual—have the power to make a difference. "What can I do to help prevent nuclear war?" Anything you want to. Taking a stand involves bringing your pro-peace or antiwar beliefs into your everyday life.

If you enjoy reaching out to people, you can take part in bridge-building activities with Soviet teens. Do you like to travel? You may be able to do that and work for peace at the same time. If you enjoy music, art, ballet, or baseball, there are ways to share them and also promote peace. Do you like politics and current affairs? Peace is an important issue for government and one way you can become involved. Issues of war and peace face you in your schoolwork right now. Asking questions and getting involved may help you in making choices about the next few years of your life.

If you've decided to become active or are thinking about it, here are some things to help you get organized.[1,2]

- Keep up with the issues. If there's one issue in which you're especially interested, learn all you can about it. Books, magazines, and newspapers are the best sources. A librarian can help you.
- Become familiar with the different points of view. Learn to tell one from the other. Separate fact from exaggeration.
- Find out if there's an active peace group or peace resource center in your area. Meet people who have been involved in peacemaking activities. Talk to them and learn from them. If you don't know anyone, ask a teacher for the name of someone involved in Educators for Social Responsibility. Or ask a member of the clergy. (You don't have to be a member of that denomination.)
- Listen to the words people use when they talk about nuclear issues. Are their facts accurate? If they appeal to the emotions, what values do they convey? Do they speak to express their opinions, to convince you, or a combination of the two? What are they leaving out? Are they open to other points of view?
- Practice peacemaking in your personal life. Try to resolve differences through discussion and understanding. Speak up for your beliefs with your friends and with adults. If you know what you're talking about, others will listen.

BRIDGE BUILDING
AND PEACE BUILDING

Bridge building between people in the U.S. and the USSR is a powerful way of working for peace. If you know someone, it's hard to think of him or her as "the enemy." School-to-school letter writing, art exchanges, and even music exchanges are taking place in many high schools. In some cases, the schools have been able to visit by satellite, using TV cameras and monitors from the local public television station.

The U.S. Information Agency and the American Council of Teachers of Russian sponsor regular exchange programs nationwide. Other organizations may also do this locally.

Going to the USSR or having Soviet students come to the U.S. is even more fun. Over and over again, American teens say about their new friends in the Soviet Union, "We have so much in common. We're so much alike." Sister school programs and special interest groups are able to visit each other more often now, as the political climate has improved. Some of them are carefully presented as "cultural exchanges" and "bridge building," not antiwar activities. Others are openly called pro-peace. It all depends on how the students see themselves. In some cases, it also depends on how their parents and school administrators view things.

Finding the money to go to the USSR is usually the biggest hurdle. Most student groups start planning a year in advance. The students save money from their own part-time jobs and also raise money as a group. Concession stands at football games, car washes, and bake sales are all popular. But adult help and money are important, too. Parents' organizations sometimes have contacts in the business

*An American student (left) greets Soviet
students arriving in the U.S. for an
exchange program. Such visits are an
excellent means of building bridges for peace.*

community who will make contributions. Some cities have "adopt-a-school" programs, where businesses provide jobs and internships for students. These interested businesses will sometimes also provide funds for an educational trip.

Visitors from the USSR can bring very little money with them, so the American students also have to raise money when the Soviet students come here. Usually, they stay in the homes of American students. In most cases the Americans pay for food, local transportation, and admission to ball games, concerts, zoos, museums, and other local attractions.

Are you thinking, "But I don't speak Russian! How will we communicate?" Language is one of the great barriers to understanding each other's cultures. Unfortunately, in the U.S. only a small number of schools teach Russian, even on the college level. In the USSR, things are different. Most students study English, and there are specialized foreign-language high schools—like magnet schools—where all the students speak English very well. It is these students who take part in the international exchanges. Even though they're part of a special group, most American students who meet them say they are typical teenagers. Some are quiet and shy; others are outgoing and adventurous. One thing they have in common is they all love rock music.

CAMPS

Even summer camp can be a pro-peace experience. There are several summer camps in both countries that bring U.S. and Soviet teens together. One in the U.S. is sponsored by the Samantha Smith Foundation, in Maine. Samantha Smith was a ten-year-old girl with a great desire for world peace. She wrote letters to the premier of the Soviet Union in the early 1980s, and was invited to visit him. Samantha became a popular ambassador for peace causes. Tragically, just a few years later, she was killed in a plane crash. In Samantha's memory, her mother began the foundation to carry on her work.

PLAYING THE PEACE GAME

You can even become better informed about world politics and the chances of nuclear war by playing games. School classes, church youth groups, and organizations are using them to increase awareness of the issues and the need for peace.

One game was invented by a nine-year-old girl, Michelle, who lives in Fresno, California. "Give Peace a Chance" is a board game, with strategy and reward cards, and peace tokens for moving around the board. Players are countries that must negotiate with each other to stay in the game.

"The Wildfire Game" was created by the Roosevelt Center for American Policy Studies, in Washington, D.C. This is a several-country scenario in which individuals or teams play the roles of nations on the brink of nuclear war. Military strategy, national interests, and negotiations all combine to determine whether the world stays at peace or vaporizes in nuclear war.

PEACE CHILD—
A MUSICAL FOR PEACE

Peace Day is the day in the year 2025 when all the nations of the world have declared peace. This is the setting for a musical for children and teens called *Peace Child* that builds bridges between the U.S. and the USSR. It tells the story of friendship that grows between an American boy and a Soviet girl as they overcome mistrust. The performances themselves are designed to do the same thing. Each cast is encouraged to add dialogue or adapt the script to its needs, as long as the message stays the same.

Children and teens have performed the play in the U.S., the USSR, China, Poland, and other countries to spread the message. Its biggest impact comes when the cast has both American and Soviet members. In some cases, both languages are used in the same performance. Cast members say this actually adds to the experience, for it proves that the message gets across in spite of language barriers. At other times, the play is performed partially live in one country and partially on tape or satellite from the other. It has been shown on public TV stations in the U.S. The entire play was broadcast on Soviet TV the day the INF Treaty was signed.

LOBBYING AND PETITIONING

One of the hallmarks of democracy is the ability to make your thoughts and ideas known to elected officials. This includes your ideas about war and peace. Public opinion is very important to elected officials. Knowing what people think helps them decide how to vote on various issues. It also helps them "keep score" on their popularity, and can persuade them to change their minds on positions they've already taken.

This applies to every official: local city council members, state legislators, governors, members of the U.S. House of Representatives and Senate, and the president. High school students are in a very good position to be extremely effective. You're young enough to attract special attention by expressing your views, and you're old enough to be registered voters in a year or two!

Keep in mind that the purpose of expressing your views is to persuade a person with power to take some action. To accomplish this, you have two major decisions to make:

• the specific issue to publicize
• how to get your message across

You should be very specific and knowledgeable about your issue. "Stopping the arms race" is too general. So is "preventing millions of deaths from nuclear war." If you choose one of the big issues, take a specific position on it, for example, "ratify the —— treaty," "begin negotiating with the Soviet Union on the subject of ——," or "don't provide money for further development of ——."

There are local "war and peace" issues in many places. Examples are the routing of trains and trucks carrying nuclear weapons through populated areas, pollution from nuclear weapons plants, and funding for U.S.-Soviet student exchange programs.

Once you decide on your issue, learn as much as you can about it. This may involve library research, reading back issues of newspapers, and talking to experts. While you're at it, find out who makes the decisions and who makes the money available for putting it into action. These are the people you want to reach.[3]

Here are various means of conveying your message:

• Coordinate a letter-writing campaign to the appropriate official. Legislators and other officials usually have a staff of people who are knowledgeable about specific issues. For each official, find out which staff member is the expert on your issue. Send him or her copies of your information or viewpoint.

• Write a letter to the editor of the local newspaper.

• Write a press release or a fact sheet and send it to all the newspapers, radio stations, and TV stations you think will be interested.

• Collect signatures on a petition and present it to the appropriate official. (Be sure to publicize that, too.) In the early 1980s, a twelve-year-old Cleveland girl named Camilla began a petition drive in favor of a freeze in the arms race. She gathered over 20,000 signatures in schools throughout the region, from the suburbs to the inner city, then sent the signed petitions to government officials in Washington.

VISITING THE NEVADA TEST SITE

The Nevada Test Site (NTS) occupies 1,400 square miles of desert that stand as a testament to the arms race. It's where weapons are tested underground (and used to be tested above ground). It's where weapons wastes are dumped. To see what nuclear explosions and radiation do, scientists recreated the bombing of Hiroshima and Nagasaki there, complete with buildings, animals, and models of human beings. It's also a tourist attraction.

Several hundred busloads of people tour the NTS each year—professional groups, peace activists, ordinary tourists. (You must be at least eighteen years old.) Each person is issued a radiation-measuring badge for the day, but the DOE says the radiation you receive, about twice the ordinary background level, is safe. The NTS is about sixty miles from Las Vegas, and the day-long escorted trips begin and end there. No cameras are allowed, but the images stay with you.

Once you're on the site, what do you see? The 140-mile circle tour starts at the Mercury operations center, where about seven thousand people work in office buildings and laboratories. Mercury is like a military base, with sleeping quarters, cafeterias and restaurants, and even a swimming pool and bowling alley. No one lives there permanently, but people often stay over during certain operations because it's so far from the city.

The control center, the command post for the explosions, is outside of Mercury. Here visitors look into the room where the test directors actually set off the explosions. They can see live TV pictures of test preparations and receive reports from monitoring equipment.

The explosions themselves take place far out in the desert, half a mile underground. If a test is under way, the site tour will continue, but visitors will be kept far away from the test hole. The DOE conducts tests of radiation effects on materials and equipment. Tests of new weapons designs are under the direction of Lawrence Livermore Laboratory, Los Alamos National Laboratory, and Sandia National Laboratory.

As the bus tour continues, the leftovers from nuclear war present a grim contrast to the ancient Joshua trees and other scenes of desert life. The visitor goes past numerous explosion craters—holes in the ground where the land has collapsed into the test hole below. Over the years, the site has experienced over eight hundred nuclear tests, so there are lots of craters to spot.

Visitors also see the now-empty pens where horses, dogs, and pigs were staked out to receive doses of radiation. In a place called Frenchman Flat, visitors drive through what was once a lifelike town, complete with lifelike human models. Now there are just a few remains of buildings, deformed by an atmospheric test more than thirty years ago. A house, a fallout shelter, a twisted railroad bridge, and even the shell of a motel are all that are left. All the others were destroyed or removed for evaluation. There's one area where tourists can't go. Nicknamed Plutonium Valley, it's too radioactive for humans even to drive past it. For information on touring the Nevada Test Site, contact Department of Energy, Nevada Operations Office, 2753 S. Highland Dr., Las Vegas, NV 89193.

PEACEFUL PUBLIC PROTESTING

Increasing the number of people who believe the way you do is an important step toward changing public policy. If you favor a test ban or arms reduction, you want to get that message to Congress and the president.

The more people who believe in your cause, the better. Politicians count noses—voters and

soon-to-be voters. The more people who see and hear your message, the better chance you have of gaining supporters. The more people who agree with you and go public about it, the more influence you have on policy-making.

Any organized protest—a march, an open meeting, or picketing—is a powerful message, especially if it's done with imagination. Signs, symbols, and costumes appeal to people's emotions, and they respond. They also make good theater and will look good on TV. The more visual your protest, the more likely it is to show up on the evening news.

You don't have to start a protest yourself. Organizations around the country are protesting for peace, usually at military bases and weapons plants. The Red River Alliance for Peace, for example, holds regular protests at the Pantex plant in Amarillo, Texas, where all nuclear weapons are assembled.

Peaceful protesting is an expression of free speech, guaranteed by the First Amendment to the Constitution. So it's entirely legal, though you may need a permit for a parade or outdoor meeting. There's also another kind of protest, called "civil disobedience."

Disarmament activists stage a "die-in" in front of the United Nations in New York, to simulate the effects of nuclear war.

CIVIL DISOBEDIENCE

Civil disobedience* is:

- Nonviolent protest.
- An act of personal commitment to an ideal or principle not fully covered by the letter of the law. A person can perform this act independently or as part of a group. Either way, the individual is responsible for his or her actions.
- Deliberately planned.
- A tactic to catch the attention of the public and the press, for instance.
- Part of a strategy to change a law or policy. It's especially aimed at lawmakers who have the power to make the change. Nuclear war is one of the most common reasons for acts of civil disobedience these days. (The others involve laws regulating abortion and immigration policies toward people trying to enter the country from Central America.)

Performing an act of civil disobedience doesn't mean the person is more committed to peace than someone who writes letters or takes part in a peaceful demonstration or a student exchange program. It's simply another way to express that commitment. Some people begin by taking part in a peaceful protest, then feel morally compelled to perform an act of civil disobedience.[4]

*Please note: "Civil disobedience" means breaking the law. People who break the law can be arrested and sent to jail. The material in this section is for you to think about and discuss.

YOU AND THE MILITARY—
DRAFT REGISTRATION

At most post offices, the rack of mailing forms also contains a large blue-and-white card. It's called a Selective Service System Registration Form, and every American man is required by law to fill one out within thirty days of his eighteenth birthday (or before his twenty-fifth birthday, if he wasn't an American earlier). The Selective Service System doesn't require much information: just your name, address, social security number, date of birth, and phone number. It also wants you to check whether you're a male or female, even though women are exempt at present.

Filling out the card does several things. Its main purpose is to register you for the military draft—requiring you to serve in the armed forces. Right now there is no draft, but Congress could enact a draft law at any time. It also makes this information available to other government agencies.

Not filling out the card makes you eligible for imprisonment for up to five years and a fine of not more than $250,000.

Congress could reactivate the draft at any time, even without a war. During times of peace, if too few young men enlist in the armed forces, the draft would provide the numbers needed. In 1988, for instance, the enlistments didn't meet the quotas set by the services. And there can be specialized drafts, for instance, of male and female health-care workers.

Also, many people believe that the voluntary enlistment plan is unfair because it appeals mostly to people from middle- and lower-income families. If war comes, they will do the fighting and dying, not people from wealthier backgrounds. The draft would share the risk more evenly.

If you don't believe in fighting, what are your choices? There are two:

• Refusal to register for the draft. This is illegal, but has been used in the past as an act of civil disobedience. Taking this step would restrict your options for the future. You could be fined and sent to jail and have a criminal record. It would be very difficult for you to obtain student aid or loans for college. You might find it easier to leave the country, but you might not be able to come back.

• Becoming a "conscientious objector." This means that you have long-standing religious or ethical objections to war and fighting and refuse to take part in it. Conscientious objection (abbreviated CO) is legal, but the law states that you must oppose "war in any form" and your belief must be deeply and firmly held. Opposition only to a particular war is not accepted.

Proving your beliefs usually requires written statements from teachers, clergy, or other people whose opinions would be respected by local draft boards. (These are groups of citizens in each community who, by law, decide who should be drafted and who should not.)

Once you receive CO status, you have two choices: You can enter the armed forces and take a "noncombatant" job, a support role that doesn't involve actual fighting, such as a medical or clerical job. Or you can perform "alternative service." This means not joining the military but working in an approved job for a social service agency for a set period of time, often several years. At present, there is no provision for conscientious objection on the draft registration forms.[5,6]

ROTC AND ENLISTMENT

Uncle Sam wants you! Maintaining defense of the U.S. depends on the armed forces having a required number of men and women, and they depend on enlistments. How do they get new recruits? They advertise. In fact, they use all the best advertising techniques to encourage you to join up.

You may have seen their ads on TV or heard them on radio. High school students are a major target for their efforts, which appear in both local and national publications aimed at teens. They may be running in your own school newspaper. A National Guard ad in the magazine *Scholastic Scope* carried a picture of combat troops with automatic weapons, with these words:

> KISS YOUR MOMMA GOOD-BYE. *No, this isn't some far-off foreign jungle. It's your own state. But these are your buddies. The guns are real. And so is the adventure. You're part of the 450,000-man backbone of American resolve: The Army National Guard. You work part time. The pay is good. True, duty in the Guard won't be the easiest way to spend a Saturday afternoon. But it will make your momma proud she raised a man.*

Another kind of military advertising is to provide classroom speakers on professional and technical topics, showing how jobs can be performed in the military as well as in civilian life. Students at one

*ROTC cadets conducting exercises.
Enlisting in the military is an
important decision that should be arrived
at only after careful consideration.*

high school recently heard a navy physician and an air force chef describe their jobs. The armed forces also appeal to your spirit of adventure with spectacular displays. "Recruitment Day" presentations at high schools may include demonstrations of tanks and other combat weapons, and even parachute jumps onto the school athletic field.

The armed forces sponsor JROTC (Junior Reserve Officers Training Corps) units at many high schools. In these, students learn military discipline and some of the ways military jobs are performed. They learn about military aspects of American history. The purpose is to encourage you to enter the service after you finish school. Even if you don't, they hope you will adopt the military's point of view, which you can support in the voting booth. You can even enlist before you finish high school and wait for up to a year before reporting for duty.

If you go to your school's counseling center, you'll find a large number of attractive brochures describing the benefits of military service. These brochures are designed to appeal to you in different ways. They promise such benefits as job training, higher education, adventure, and travel. Many young people have indeed gained these things from the military, but the realities of being in the armed services are not always what the brochures and recruiters say they are. You may not be able to use your military training in civilian life because comparable jobs don't exist. You may not get the training you were promised when you enlisted. The military doesn't have to assign you to a job in the field for which you are trained. There may not be openings, or the service may need you for other duties.

Military discipline is very strict, and you will be

subject to it twenty-four hours a day. Your freedom to speak out and to state your beliefs will be limited. Military justice is separate from the civilian court systems, and in some cases you can be punished without a trial or the help of a lawyer.

One pacifist organization has these suggestions for talking to a recruiter and considering enlistment:

• Before you go, ask yourself: When would you be willing to get involved in a conflict? Which weapons or methods could you use in good conscience— nuclear? chemical or biological? self-defense? nonviolent? Whom are you willing to fight as the enemy— anyone the government says? soldiers on the other side? civilians? no one?

• Don't go alone. Take a witness in case the recruiter makes promises the service doesn't live up to.

• Don't sign any enlistment papers on the spot. Take them home with you and read them carefully. Be sure you understand everything in the papers before you sign.

• Get all promises of particular training or assignments in writing. Spoken promises aren't binding on the armed forces. Keep copies of all the papers you sign.

• Ask these questions: How long is my enlistment? Do I have to meet special physical requirements for the job I want? Are there other requirements? What happens if I don't meet the requirements? What happens if I don't complete the training for special programs? Will my assignment to a particular base be for my entire enlistment period?[4–6]

Recruiting efforts, displays, ROTC, and the Armed Services Vocational Aptitude Battery

(ASVAB, a widely used standardized test) give the Armed Forces a strong presence at most high schools. You can make a statement for peace to go alongside of it.

Many peace organizations have information describing peace-and-justice-related jobs that provide travel and adventure and also help improve people's lives. But schools don't have it. You can ask your counseling center to make this information available.

Sometimes taking a stand at school for peace is difficult. Several years ago, a group of students and adults in one suburb wanted to place an antidraft advertisement in the local high school newspaper. The ad showed a ghostly figure saying, "Don't let the draft blow you away."

The school administration wouldn't allow the ad to run, saying the group was advocating an illegal activity. The students said their freedom of speech was being violated. After several years of negotiation and lawsuits, the school district agreed to allow the antidraft ads if they met general guidelines for student publications.

WHEN YOU HAVE MONEY

Taking a stand against nuclear war and for peace is something that can become part of your whole way of life. Take the way you manage your money. One of the ways people make their money work for them is to put it in bank accounts or invest it in the stocks and bonds of corporations. If a company's shares are bought and sold on the stock market, information is available about the products it makes and where it does business. There are lots of banks and other companies to invest in, so it's possible to select companies whose products and policies you approve of or want to avoid. This approach is called "socially responsible investing."

Some people use this strategy to avoid investing in nuclear power, the defense industry, or other products, such as tobacco and liquor. Others use it to invest in companies whose activities (social goals, environmental protection record, or actions in various foreign countries, etc.) meet their approval. There are also "socially responsible" mutual funds, which are packages of investments in different companies.

People who invest this way usually make just as much money from their investments as people who don't, so you don't make a financial sacrifice by investing responsibly. Where can you get information about these investments? Most public libraries have a series of books called Standard & Poor's guides to corporations. Many religious denominations have offices for social responsibility and may have information. Also, many large stock brokerage firms and individual brokers have lists of socially responsible companies and mutual funds. Or you can tell them what you want or don't want, and ask them to find investments that meet your own needs. Peace organizations also have lists of major defense contractors.

NINE

YOUNG PEOPLE WHO TOOK A STAND

How do people your age speak out against war and for peace? Here are the statements of just a few of them.

MICHAELYN—
A STUDENT LEADER

Michaelyn went to the USSR with a peace organization, and has founded a student chapter at her high school.

What I really want to do is get kids in my school involved in exchanges. I want my school to be a sister school. Raising money will be a problem, because it's a private Catholic school, and they don't allow fund-raisers. But I think we should get more involved in international issues. So many kids want to go to the Soviet Union. I want to share the same experience that I had with other teenagers. I learned so much.

We're writing individual letters to the president and to Gorbachev. We think handwritten letters are more effective than mass-produced ones.

Basically, I think the only way to have peace is to have better personal relations between the superpowers.

After I came back from the Soviet Union, I didn't think war was as big of a threat to me. I think if we can share life-styles and be able to see the way they live there and how loving they are, people won't feel so threatened. This may not solve the problems of nuclear war, but it makes people feel a little more peaceful.

I'm applying to colleges now, and I'm thinking about studying foreign relations, because of all this. Now I'm so interested in the whole thing! It's an experience that I've learned so much from and that will be part of the rest of my life.

ANDREW—
A BRIDGE BUILDER

Andrew was a sophomore when he helped create a cultural exchange program at his public high school: "There were so many stereotypes and misconceptions separating the Soviets and the Americans. Adults had a growing forum for discussion, and adults were doing all the planning. But youth really hadn't had a chance."

After Andrew and his friends developed their plan, they found a faculty member to sponsor them. Their efforts have allowed an exchange of visits with a sister school in Moscow. While in the Soviet Union, they took part in an international camp where students from both countries wrote a resolution to be sent to the leaders of the two nations. It says, in part:

It should be noted that the youth of the world are greatly appreciative of the positive relations between our nations but are very concerned with the problems and differences on this earth and want to offer our aid in solving these problems and creating public awareness about these issues.

Here are some of their suggestions:

- "Peaceland," a dual facility in the United States and the Soviet Union, as international peace education and cooperation centers.
- Youth art and cultural exchanges . . . for promoting the understanding of the history, culture, and traditions of our two peoples.
- An annual student folklore festival and the exchange of applied arts, crafts, and films.

CHRIS—
A MUSICIAN FOR PEACE

Chris, a high school student, is a rock musician. He went to the Soviet Union for the first time with a group of students from his school and took tapes of his rock group with him. The music made a big hit with Soviet teens. As a result, Chris was invited back, along with his group, to play a series of concerts. He saw going to the Soviet Union with his classmates as more than an educational experience. It was a special opportunity.

It became a personal commitment and the beginning of a life that I wanted to have dedicated to peace. So for me that was a beginning. I made some great friends in the Soviet Union. My trip was a great experience. The world seems a lot smaller to me now that I have friends there. The trip went beyond my expectations. It was just won-

derful. I expected people to be nice, and I expected them to greet us the way they did, which was like brothers and sisters. I expected people to be the same as people here. But I guess I didn't really expect to enjoy the Soviet Union—the country—as much as I did.

We've gotten friendships out of the trip that are very important to me. Things are happening from it, which is positive. The trip was an effort to build a relationship that would lead to coexistence.

Going back with the band is like a reward for my commitment, and it's going to be the continuation of my commitment. And I'm getting more people involved, too.

The band also sees it as a great opportunity to break down barriers between our two countries. We're excited about our first opportunity to travel to the Soviet Union. But we're already involved in Amnesty International and we've done a lot of things for local organizations. So it's a socially conscious group.

We expect to play about 20 concerts on college campuses and community centers, with crowds between 300 and 1,000. And in Moscow and Leningrad.

ERIC—
A WAR PROTESTOR

There are two ways to enter the Nevada Test Site. One is on a tour bus. The other is on foot, as an act of civil disobedience. The NTS has become a rallying point for people who want to protest our present nuclear policy.

The NTS is located in Nye County, Nevada, and the county is in charge of law enforcement outside the site, where protestors gather. People who stay outside the site can remain for their rally. Those who cross the line onto the site are arrested by the Nye County sheriff's deputies. The act has become very much of a ritual.

Eric, now a college student, began protesting the development of nuclear weapons when he was sixteen, by taking part in demonstrations at the NTS. Since then, he has been part of six demonstrations. He was arrested once as a part of his commitment.

My first demonstration was in 1986. I didn't know what to expect. I expected it to be more radical than I think it was. You go up there the first time, and you're committed.

The demonstrators are incredibly warm. They understand. It's a great thing, because there're people from all different places, different types of societies, different beliefs, different religions. And they're all there for one reason. It doesn't matter where you came from or what color you are or what you're wearing. You're there for a purpose, because something's being done that's wrong to everybody.

The protest was on Mahatma Gandhi's birthday, and I went up with my girlfriend, with the full intent to get arrested. That was my first time up there since I turned eighteen, so I could get arrested without hassling my parents. That's why I waited.

If you're going to get arrested, it's really smart to have a support group. They do take you to jail. So you need someone to make phone calls and make bail for you, and be there on the outside. We got up there at eleven at night and sat by a fire with other people from Alliance for Survival. The next morning we asked them if they would be our support. They were so much support it was unbelievable. We were among the first to get arrested that day.

Getting arrested is—it's amazing! It's an incredible feeling; it's just surrendering everything you have toward your conviction. I didn't know what I would feel—I really didn't. It's so much stronger than protesting, actually giving yourself over to the powers for whatever they want to do. It doesn't matter, because you're so sure of your conviction. It was a great thing. I'm planning to do it again.

It's a terrible thing that getting arrested is the only way you can make noise and actually be heard—and I don't even know if they really listen. People get arrested at every protest. And there're people who get arrested five times a day. It's gotten to be a routine. They just process you and you're out. Nye County is not pressing charges anymore, which is good for the people protesting, but it's also bad, because it doesn't make noise. They've even built the jail cells on the site. You climb the fence or walk across the barrier and they have the pens right there. You're thrown in and processed out within two or three hours.

It's a shame that you have to break the law to make noise. It's a shame that the government won't even listen to you. It's like they could care less.

To change things, you have to make a long-term commitment. If organizations try to do things in two or three years, nothing's ever going to happen.

MIGUEL—
A HIGH SCHOOL PEACE ACTIVIST

Miguel, now in college, was one of the high school students involved in the antidraft ad controversy. He has said:

I was always angered that my school glorified its navy JROTC program and boasted about the fact that we had been "adopted" by the navy—meaning the school receives money from the navy in exchange for plastering our campus with military recruiting propaganda.

The years one spends in high school are some of the most important in a person's life. It is a time when we take *conscientious stands on several issues, when learning coincides with deciding. It is also a time when we are faced with the option of joining the military, which "promises" a safe, planned-out future, or venturing out into an unknown future which promises little, but almost certain unemployment. This is the picture that the military's $1-billion-a-year recruiting campaign tries to create.*

A FINAL THOUGHT

Your life is what you make of it. The earth's future is what we all make of it. Basing your life on peace may be one of the best ways of living it—for you and the earth.

Pax. Shalom. Peace. Mir.

A PARTIAL DIRECTORY OF PEACE ORGANIZATIONS

American Field Service
International Intercultural Programs
313 E. 43rd St.
New York, NY 10017

American Friends Service Committee
Peace Education Division
1501 Cherry St.
Philadelphia, PA 19102

American Jewish Congress
Task Force on Nuclear Disarmament
72 Franklin St., Room 402
Boston, MA 02110

Catholic Peace Fellowship
339 Lafayette St.
New York, NY 10012

Central Committee for Conscientious Objectors
2208 South St.
Philadelphia, PA 19146

Children's Campaign for Nuclear Disarmament
14 Everit St.
New Haven, CT 06511

Council for a Livable World
20 Park Plaza
Boston, MA 02166

Educators for Social Responsibility
23 Garden St.
Cambridge, MA 02138

Evangelicals for Social Action
712 G St., SE
Washington, DC 20003

Fellowship of Reconciliation
P.O. Box 271
Nyack, NY 10960

Greenpeace USA
1611 Connecticut Ave., NW
Washington, DC 20009

International Student Pugwash
505B 2nd St., NE
Washington, DC 20002

Jobs with Peace Campaign
76 Summer St.
Boston, MA 02110

Mothers Embracing Nuclear Disarmament (MEND)
P.O. Box 2309
La Jolla, CA 92038

National Interreligious Service Board
for Conscientious Objectors
800 18th St., NW, Suite 600
Washington, DC 20006

Pax Christi USA
348 E. 10th St.
Erie, PA 16503

Physicians for Social Responsibility
639 Massachusetts Ave.
Cambridge, MA 02139

Red River Alliance for Peace
1605 Westside
Sherman, TX 75090

SANE/FREEZE
711 G St., SE
Washington, DC 20003

Union of Concerned Scientists
26 Church St.
Cambridge, MA 02238

Unitarian Universalist Peace Network
5808 Greene St.
Philadelphia, PA 19144

Women's International League for Peace and Freedom
710 G St., SE
Washington, DC 20003

OTHER SOURCES OF INFORMATION

Bulletin of the Atomic Scientists
Monthly magazine devoted to nuclear issues

Center for Defense Information
1500 Massachusetts Ave., NW
Washington, DC 20005

Peace Works, Inc. ("Give Peace a Chance" game)
3812 N. First St.
Fresno, CA 93726

Peace Child Foundation
3977 Chain Bridge Rd.
Fairfax, VA 22030

Project on Youth and Non-Military Opportunities
(Project YANO)
P.O. Box 157
Encinitas, CA 92024

Roosevelt Center for American Policy Studies
316 Pennsylvania Ave., SE, Suite 500
Washington, DC 20003

Samantha Smith Foundation
9 Union St.
Hallowell, ME 04347

U.S.-USSR High School Academic Partnership Program
U.S. Information Agency
c/o American Council of Teachers of Russian
1619 Massachusetts Ave., NW
Washington, DC 20036

For touring the Nevada Test Site, contact:
Department of Energy
Nevada Operations Office
2753 S. Highland Dr.
Las Vegas, NV 89193

Please note: Peace organizations are usually nonprofit. If you write to these organizations for information or materials, ask if they charge a fee. Also, enclose a stamped envelope.

NOTES

CHAPTER ONE
WHAT NUCLEAR WAR MEANS

1. Ruth Adams and Susan Cullen, *The Final Epidemic: Physicians and Scientists on Nuclear War* (Chicago: Educational Foundation for Nuclear Science, 1981).
2. *Ambio.* Special Issue on Nuclear War. Volume 11, No. 2–3, 1982.
3. Eric Chivian et al., eds., *Last Aid: The Medical Dimensions of Nuclear War* (San Francisco: W. H. Freeman and Company, 1982).
4. William C. Roesch, ed., *U.S.-Japan Joint Reassessment of Atomic Bomb Radiation Dosimetry in Hiroshima and Nagasaki.* Final Report. Vol. 1: Dosimetry System 1986 (DS86). Radiation Effects Research Foundation 1987.
5. Dept. of Political and Security Council Affairs. United Nations Centre for Disarmament, *Report of the Secretary-General. Comprehensive Study on Nuclear Weapons.* United Nations. 1981.
6. Office of Technology Assessment, *The Effects of Nuclear War.* Washington, DC, 1979.
7. Paul Ehrlich, Carl Sagan, Donald Kennedy, Walter Orr Roberts, *The Cold and the Dark. The World After Nuclear War* (New York: W.W. Norton, 1984).
8. Thomas Piemonte, "Nuclear Winter," The *Lancet* 10-1-88, p. 785.

CHAPTER TWO
HOW NUCLEAR WEAPONS WORK

1. Samuel Glasstone and Philip J. Dolan, eds., *The Effects of Nuclear Weapons* (U.S. Department of Defense and ERDA, 1977).
2. Ruth Adams and Susan Cullen, *The Final Epidemic: Physicians and Scientists on Nuclear War* (Chicago: Educational Foundation for Nuclear Science, 1981).
3. Eric Chivian et al., eds., *Last Aid: The Medical Dimensions of Nuclear War* (San Francisco: W. H. Freeman and Company, 1982).
4. William C. Roesch, ed., *U.S.-Japan Joint Reassessment of Atomic Bomb Radiation Dosimetry in Hiroshima and Nagasaki*. Final Report. Vol. 1: Dosimetry System 1986 (DS86). Radiation Effects Research Foundation 1987.
5. U.S. Dept. of Energy, *Environmental Survey*. Preliminary Summary Report of the Defense Production Facilities. DOE/EH-0072. Sept. 1988.
6. Tom Gervasi, *Arsenal of Democracy II. American Military Power in the 1980s and the Origins of the New Cold War* (New York: Grove Press, 1981).

CHAPTER THREE THE COLD WAR—
FORTY YEARS OF MAD

1. Herbert F. York, *Making Weapons, Talking Peace* (New York: Basic Books, 1987).
2. "East-West Friction: The NATO Years," *New York Times* 5-29-89, p. A4.
3. U.S. Arms Control and Disarmament Agency, *Arms Control and Disarmament Agreements*, 1980 ed.
4. Jerome B. Wiesner, "The Glory and Tragedy of the Partial Test Ban," *New York Times* 4-11-88, p. 25.
5. U.S. Dept. of Defense, *Soviet Military Power 1985* (Washington, DC: U.S. Government Printing Office).
6. George F. Kennan, "After the Cold War," *New York Times Magazine* 2-5-89, p. 32.
7. Richard M. Nixon, "America Must Keep Pressure on the Kremlin," *San Diego Union* 3-26-89, p. C-1.

CHAPTER FOUR
PROLIFERATION AND THE CHANCE OF WAR

1. Lynn E. Davis, "Lessons of the INF Treaty," *Foreign Affairs,* Spring 1988, p. 720.
2. Lawrence Scheinman, "The IAEA at Thirty." *Resources,* Winter 1988 (Washington: Resources for the Future, p. 16).
3. Michael R. Gordon, "Norway Is Missing Atom Arms Water," *New York Times* 5-5-88, p. 1; "Norway Says a Second Shipment of Heavy Water May Be Missing," *New York Times* 5-25-88, p. 4; "Oslo Says Atom Water Was Diverted to India," *New York Times* 11-4-88, p. A8.
4. Sanjoy Hazarika, "Norway Details How Heavy Water For Use in a Bomb Went to India," *New York Times* 5-7-89, p. A12.
5. "Missiles in small nations called threat. Institute declares Cold War over, but other perils persist," *San Diego Union* 5-25-89, p. A-20 (AP).
6. Oscar Arias Sanchez, "To Mr. Gorbachev: Stop Sending Arms," *New York Times* 3-3-88, p. 27.
7. Caspar W. Weinberger, "Arms Reductions and Deterrence," *Foreign Affairs,* Spring 1988, p. 700.
8. Gary Milhollin, "New Nuclear Follies?" *New York Times* 11-25-87, p. 27.

CHAPTER FIVE
PROTECTING THE UNITED STATES

1. Gordon Adams, *The Politics of Defense Contracting: The Iron Triangle* (New Brunswick: Transaction Books, 1982).
2. Ruth Leger Sivard, *World Military and Social Expenditures 1987–1988.* 12th ed. (Washington, DC: World Priorities, 1987).
3. Sidney D. Drell and Thomas H. Johnson, "Managing Strategic Weapons," *Foreign Affairs,* Summer 1988, p. 1027.
4. Union of Concerned Scientists, *Briefing Papers:* "Command and Control of Strategic Forces." "MX and Midgetman Missiles." "Nuclear Proliferation." "Nuclear Weapons Testing."
5. Michael Brower, "Cancel the Stealth Bomber," *New York Times* 5-19-77, p. 27.
6. "Stealth Bomber Due to Fly in Fall," *New York Times* 4-21-88, p. 10

7. Philip M. Boffey, et al., *Claiming the Heavens: The New York Times Complete Guide to the Star Wars Debate* (New York: Times Books, 1988).
8. "Catastrophic Failure predicted for Star Wars," *San Diego Union* 4-24-88, p. A-2.
9. Louis Deschamps, *The SDI and European Security Interests.* Atlantic Paper No. 62. The Atlantic Institution for International Affairs. n.d.
10. Michael R. Gordon, "Bush Plans to Cut Reagan Requests for Key Weapons" [Star Wars Chronology], *New York Times* 4-24-89, p. 1.
11. Colin Norman, "SDI: Testing the Limits," *Science* 1-15-88, p. 246.
12. Edward Teller, "X-Ray Laser: A Key to SDI," *San Diego Union* 2-14-88, p. C-1.
13. "U.S. Could Use 'Star Wars' as Cover for Nuclear Weapons, Soviet Says," *San Diego Union* 7-14-88, p. A-4.

CHAPTER SIX
REDUCING THE NUCLEAR ARSENALS

1. George F. Kennan, "After the Cold War," *New York Times Magazine* 2-5-89, p. 32.
2. Richard M. Nixon, "America Must Keep Pressure on the Kremlin," *San Diego Union* 3-26-89, p. C-1.
3. Lynn E. Davis, "Lessons of the INF Treaty," *Foreign Affairs,* Spring 1988, p. 720.
4. Frank J. Gaffney, Jr., "This Is Arms Control?" *New York Times* 5-10-88, p. 31.
5. Adm. Gene R. LaRoque, Kenneth Adelman, E.R. Zumwalt, Jr., Gerard C. Smith, R. Emmett Tyrrell, Jr., Ted Galen Carpenter, Thomas Moorer, and Gwynne Dyer, "What Is Ours to Defend?" *Harper's Magazine,* July 1988, pp. 39–50.
6. Stansfield Turner, "Winnowing Our Warheads," *New York Times Magazine* 3-27-88, p. 46.
7. Stansfield Turner, "Arm for the Real Threats," *New York Times* 4-10-89, p. A15.
8. Jeffrey Record and David B. Rivkin, Jr., "Defending Post-INF Europe," *Foreign Affairs,* Spring 1988, p. 735.
9. Zbigniew Brzezinski, "America's New Geostrategy," *Foreign Affairs,* Spring 1988, p. 680.

10. Herbert F. York, *Making Weapons, Talking Peace* (New York: Basic Books, 1987).
11. Sandra Blakeslee, "Method to Verify Arms Ban Is Tested by U.S. and Soviet," *New York Times* 4-30-88, p. 4.
12. Harold A. Feiveson, Christopher E. Paine, Frank von Hippel, "A Low-Threshold Test Ban Is Feasible," *Science* 2-23-87, p. 455.
13. Harold A. Feiveson and Robert H. Williams, "Putting a Lock on Plutonium," *New York Times* 5-28-88, p. 15.
14. J. C. Mark, et al., "The Tritium Factor as a Forcing Function in Nuclear Arms Reduction Talks," *Science* 9-2-88, p. 1166.
15. W. G. Sutcliffe, "Limits on Nuclear Materials for Arms Reduction: Complexities and Uncertainties," *Science* 9-2-88, p. 1166.
16. U.S. Arms Control and Disarmament Agency, *Arms Control and Disarmament Agreements,* 1980 ed.

CHAPTER SEVEN
PEACE, PEACE ADVOCATES, AND SOCIAL JUSTICE

1. William James, *The Varieties of Religious Experience. A Study in Human Nature* (New York: Modern Library, 1936).
2. Charles DeBeneditti, ed., *Peace Heroes in Twentieth-Century America* (Bloomington: Indiana University Press, 1986).
3. Arthur and Lila Weinberg, eds., *Instead of Violence* (New York: Grossman Publishers, 1963).
4. Robert Heyer, ed., *Nuclear Disarmament. Key Statements of Popes, Bishops, Councils and Churches* (New York: Paulist Press, 1982).
5. R. J. Sider and D. J. Brubaker, eds., *Preaching on Peace* (Philadelphia: Fortress Press, 1982).
6. The Bible. Various translations.
7. James Hastings, ed., *Encyclopedia of Religion and Ethics* (New York: Charles Scribner's Sons, n.d.).

CHAPTER EIGHT
TAKING A STAND

1. Educators for Social Responsibility, *Dialogue. A Teaching Guide to Nuclear Issues* (Cambridge, MA: Educators for Social Responsibility, 1982).

2. David Krieger and Frank Kelly, eds., *Waging Peace in the Nuclear Age* (Santa Barbara, CA: Capra Press, 1988).
3. Donald deKieffer, *How to Lobby Congress* (New York: Dodd, Mead, 1981).
4. Project YANO. *It's Not Just a Job. It's Eight Years of Your Life* (Project on Youth and Nonmilitary Opportunities, Encinitas, CA).
5. Stephen Markham, "Nuclear War: Teaching Manual for the Challenge of Peace." Chap. 7. *Social Justice* (Winona, MN: St. Mary's Press, Christian Brothers Publications, 1985).
6. Thomas Matty and the Peace Studies Task Force. *A Ten-Session Unit: Peace and Conscience Formation* (Winona, MN: St. Mary's Press, Christian Brothers Publications, 1985).

GLOSSARY

Air burst. The detonation of a weapon above the ground rather than at ground level.

Chain reaction. A sustained and increasing series of nuclear fissions, as in a reactor or weapon.

Critical mass. The amount of fissionable material required for a nuclear explosion to take place.

Cruise missile. A small jet-powered maneuverable missile for use in either strategic or tactical situations.

Deterrence. A strategy to prevent war that depends on each side knowing that the two sides can destroy each other. The long-standing official policy of the United States. (See also MAD.)

Deuterium. An isotope of hydrogen containing one proton and one neutron. It is used in some kinds of nuclear weapons.

Dose. An amount of radiation. Absorbed dose is the amount received by living tissue, measured as rem or rad.

Electron. A negatively charged particle. Electrons form the outer layer of atoms.

EM pulse. A series of radio waves generated by a nuclear explosion. Experts believe that EM pulses will disable electrical and electronic equipment during a nuclear war.

Fallout. Radioactive materials carried into the atmosphere because of a nuclear explosion. They eventually drop back to earth, contaminating air, water, and soil and threatening the health of humans, other animals, and plants.

Fireball. A mass of air heated to millions of degrees by the explosion of a nuclear weapon.

First-strike capability. Possession of enough nuclear weaponry to achieve a military victory and destroy an enemy's ability to strike back.

Fission. A reaction that splits the nuclei of uranium-235 or plutonium-239, releasing energy.

Fission products. Radioactive isotopes created as the result of a fission reaction.

Fusion. A reaction that releases energy by fusing the nuclei of two hydrogen atoms.

Gamma ray. A form of ionizing radiation emitted by various isotopes, similar to X rays.

Geosynchronous orbit. The orbit of a satellite that moves at the same speed as the earth's rotation. This keeps the satellite over the same point on earth at all times.

Grey. Unit of radiation dose used in most parts of the world; 1 grey = 100 rads.

Ground zero. The place where a nuclear weapon is detonated.

Half-life. The amount of time it takes a radioactive substance to lose half of its radioactivity.

ICBM. Intercontinental ballistic missile. A strategic weapon.

Ionizing radiation. Energy from natural or engineered sources that affects living tissue by disrupting its atoms, stripping the electrons from the nuclei.

Isotope. A variation of an element, depending on the number of neutrons in the nucleus.

Kiloton (kT). A measure of explosive power equal to 1 thousand tons of TNT.

Launch on warning. Launching of nuclear weapons upon receiving a signal that enemy weapons have been launched. It may be automated, omitting human decision making.

MAD. Mutually assured destruction. The policy of deterrence in which war is prevented because each side knows that either side can destroy the other.

Megaton (MT). A measure of explosive power equal to 1 million tons of TNT.

MIRV. Multiple independently targetable reentry vehicle. Multi-warhead missiles are known as "MIRVs."

Neutron. A neutrally charged particle found in the nucleus of an atom. Neutrons are used to start fission reactions. When released during a nuclear explosion, they can do biological damage.

NORAD. North American Air Defense Command. The military group in charge of launching nuclear weapons.

Nucleus (pl: nuclei). The core or center of an atom, held together by energy. The nuclei of certain atoms can be split, releasing energy. Those of other atoms can be fused, also releasing energy.

Overpressure. The pressure above normal atmospheric pressure created by a nuclear explosion.

Plutonium. A created element, not found in nature, containing ninety-four protons. Plutonium-239 is fissionable and radioactive; it is created in a nuclear reactor from uranium-238.

Proton. A positively charged particle found in the nucleus of an atom. The number of protons in a nucleus determine the element.

Rad. A measurement of radiation dose in terms of energy absorbed by tissue. One rad equals 100 ergs of radiation per gram of body tissue.

Radiation sickness. A set of health problems caused by an overdose of ionizing radiation. Depending on the dose, a person may recover or may die.

Rem. A measurement of radiation dose that considers the behavior of different types of radiation in tissue as well as the energy absorbed by the tissue (rad).

Safeguards. Inspections and other guarantees under the International Atomic Energy Agency or other international agencies to prevent use of civilian nuclear power for military purposes.

Seismic. The disturbance of the earth following an earthquake or underground weapon explosion.

SLBM. Submarine-launched ballistic missile: a strategic weapon.

Strategic nuclear weapon. A weapon that travels long distances, such as between the U.S. and the USSR.

Tactical nuclear weapon. A weapon that travels within a continent, nation, or smaller geographic area.

Thermonuclear reaction. A nuclear reaction, such as a fusion reaction, requiring high temperatures to take place.

Triad. The three methods of launching nuclear weapons—airplanes, landbased missile launchers, and oceangoing missile launchers.

Tritium. A radioactive isotope of hydrogen containing one proton and two neutrons. It is used in thermonuclear weapons.

Uranium. A natural element whose nucleus contains ninety-two protons. One of its isotopes, U-235, is fissionable and used in nuclear weapons. Another isotope, U-238, is used to produce plutonium.

Verification. Inspections and other procedures to prove that all parties to an agreement are living up to it.

Warhead. The explosive portion of a weapon. A nuclear warhead contains materials to produce fission and/or fusion reactions.

Yield. The explosive power of a nuclear weapon, in megatons, for example.

FOR FURTHER
READING

Adams, Ruth, and Cullen, Susan, eds. *The Final Epidemic. Physicians and Scientists on Nuclear War.* Chicago: Education Foundation for Nuclear Science, 1981. Description of the health effects of nuclear war

Chivian, Eric, et al., eds. *Last Aid. The Medical Dimensions of Nuclear War.* New York: W. H. Freeman and Company, 1982. Also on the health effects of nuclear war

Conetta, Carl, ed. *Peace Resource Book: A Comprehensive Guide to Issues, Groups, and Literature.* Cambridge, MA: Ballinger, 1988. Contains listing of thousands of peace organizations in the U.S.

DeBenedetti, Charies, ed. *Peace Heroes in Twentieth-Century America.* Bloomington: Indiana University Press, 1986. Biographies of peace advocates

The Words of Martin Luther King, Jr. New York: Newmarket Press, 1987. Selected and introduced by Coretta Scott King. Statements on peace and social action by the civil rights leader

Meltzer, Milton. *Ain't Gonna Study War No More.* New York: Harper and Row, 1985. History of peacemaking

Meyer, Ethel Patterson. *Champions of Peace.* Boston: Little Brown, 1959. Stories of winners of the Nobel Peace Prize

Pirtle, Sarah. *An Outbreak of Peace*. Philadelphia: New Society Publishers, 1987. Novel about teens who start a peace group

Questions & Answers on the Soviet Threat and National Security. Philadelphia: American Friends Service Committee, n.d. Booklet answering commonly asked questions about peace and security

Sider, Ronald J., and Brubaker, Darrel J. *Preaching on Peace*. Philadelphia: Fortress Press, 1982. Statements on peace by various Roman Catholic and Protestant clergy

U.S. Arms Control and Disarmament Agency. *Arms Control and Disarmament Agreements*. Washington, D.C., current edition. Texts of treaties and histories of negotiations

INDEX

Electrons, 31, 36, 39
El Salvador, 47, 74
Emerson, Ralph Waldo,
107–8
Energy, 31, 33, 51
Energy Department, U.S.
(DOE), 40, 69, 130
Enlistment, 137–41, 148–49
Enriched uranium fuel, 69–70
Environment, 28
Epicenter, 13–15, 39
Exchange programs, 123–25,
124, 128, 143, 144
Explosions, 13–15, 16–17, 37

Fallout, 15–21, *19*, 28, 39, 55,
58
Fat Man, 30, 34, 40
Fires, 15, 24–25, 37
First strikes, 50, 82, 83, 87–
88, 103
Fission weapons, 30, 33–36
France, 37, 52, 58, 60–61, 64,
71, 72
Fuels, 34–36, 69–70
Fusion weapons, 30, 36–37

Games, pro-peace, 126
Gamma radiation, 38–39
Gandhi, Mohandas, 104, 110–
12, 115
Genetic damage, 28, 38
Germany, East, 74, 91
Germany, Nazi, 48–52, 72,
91, 105, 112
Germany, West, 71, 74, 101
"Give Peace a Chance," 126
Gorbachev, Mikhail, *65*, 66,
143
Graham, Billy, 117, 118
Great Britain, 52, 55, 60,
110–12

Ground zero, 13–15, 39

Heavy water (deuterium ox-
ide), 69, 70–71
Helium, 36, 39
Hiroshima bombing (1945),
18–21, 23, 30, 37, 49, 129
Hitler, Adolf, 48, 49, 91, 105,
112
Hot line, 58
Hydrogen, 31, *32*, 36
Hydrogen bombs (H-bombs),
30, 36–37, 55, 114

India, 59, 69, 72, 74, 110–12
Indian wars (1870s–90s), 104
Induced radioactivity, 39
Intercontinental ballistic mis-
siles (ICBMs), 40–43, 63,
72, 80, 82, 96, 101, 102,
103
Interim Agreement (1972),
62, 63
Intermediate Nuclear-Range
Force (INF) Treaty (1987),
65, 66, 93, 94, 97, 101, 102,
103, 127
International Atomic Energy
Agency (IAEA), 59, 60, 61,
67, 71, 73
International Labor Organiza-
tion, 110
International Physicians for
the Prevention of Nuclear
War, 108–9
Investing, socially responsible,
141–42
Ionizing radiation, 39
Iran, 59, 72, 74, 105
Iraq, 72, 74, 105
Iron Triangle, 77, 79
Islam, 120

170

Non-proliferation Treaty
(1968), 60–61, 64, 67–69,
73
North American Air Defense
Command (NORAD), 75
North Atlantic Treaty Organization (NATO), 76, 92, 97,
101, 103
Norway, 71
Nuclear energy, 31, 51
Nuclear reactors, 59–60, 69–
70
accidents at, 18, 24
Nuclear Test Ban Readiness
Program, 98
Nuclear war, 13–29
explosions in, 13–15, 16–
17
fatalities in, *14*, 15, 18,
19, 20, 23
first year after, 24–26
long-term consequences
of, 27–29
radiation sickness after,
21–24
radioactive fallout in, 15–
21, *19*, 28
reasons to oppose, 115–
16
scenarios for, 74–75
Nuclear winter, 24–26
Nuclei, 31, 39

Offensive weapons:
defensive weapons vs., 80,
95
new, 80–83, *81, 84*
Office of Technology Assessment, 87, 99
Ohio, 44
Outer Space Treaty (1967),
58, 88

Ozone layer, 27

Pacifism, 104–5
Pakistan, 59, 69, 72, 74
Partial Test Ban Treaty
(1963), 58, 62, 99
Peace, 12, 105–6
Peace advocacy, 104–49
Bible and, 117, 118–19
bridge building in, 123–
25, *124*, 127, 144–45
camps in, 125–26
civil disobedience in, 134,
136, 146–48
draft registration and,
135–37, 141
early examples of, 106–8
in early twentieth cen-
tury, 108–12
games in, 126
Judeo-Christian beliefs
and, 116–18
lobbying and petitioning
in, 127–29
musical for, 126–27
Nevada Test Site visits in,
129–31, 146–48
in nuclear age, 112–15
peaceful public protesting
in, 131–33, *132*
personal statements
about, 143–49
and reasons for opposing
nuclear war, 115–16
socially responsible investing in, 141–42
tips for, 122
Peace Child, 126–27
Peaceful Nuclear Explosives
Treaty (1976), 63
Peaceful public protesting,
131–33, *132*

ABOUT
THE AUTHOR

Ellen Thro is a free-lance writer specializing in science, technology, and medicine. In addition to her numerous books and magazine articles, she has also written classroom audiovisual materials. Ms. Thro is a graduate of Smith College and currently resides in San Diego, California. She is also the author of *Robotics Careers,* another Franklin Watts book.